Junior Maths

3

Asit Das Gupta
Anindita Banerjee

Bharati Bhawan
PUBLISHERS & DISTRIBUTORS

Published by
BHARATI BHAWAN (Publishers & Distributors)
www.bharatibhawan.in   email: editorial@bbpd.in

4271/3 Ansari Road, Daryaganj, NEW DELHI 110 002, Phone: 23286557
A-61 B/2 Sector 63, NOIDA 201 307, Phone: 4757400
Thakurbari Road, PATNA 800 003, Phone: 2670325
10 Raja Subodh Mallick Square, KOLKATA 700 013, Phone: 22250651
No. 98 Sirsi Circle, Mysore Road, BENGALURU 560 018, Phone: 26740560

First edition 2010
2020 reprint

Illustrations: Kallol Majumder

Junior Maths 3
Printed at Nutech Print Services-India, Faridabad

CONTENTS

1. Review of Numbers up to 999

We use the digits 0, 1, 2, 3, 4, 5, 6, 7, 8 and 9 to write numbers.
Numbers have one or more digits.
Numbers like 0, 3, 6 and 8 have just one digit. They are one-digit numbers.
Numbers like 10, 19, 52 and 97 are two-digit numbers.
100, 207, 563, 729 and 987 are some three-digit numbers.

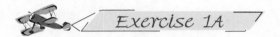
Exercise 1A

Fill in.

The smallest one-digit number is 0. The largest (greatest) one-digit number is _9_ .
The largest two-digit number is 99. The smallest two-digit number is _10_.
The smallest three-digit number is _100_. The greatest three-digit number is _999_.

Write 461 to 480.

461	462	463	464	465	466	467	468	469	470
471	472	473	474	475	476	477	478	479	480

Write 891 to 910.

891	892	893	894	895	896	897	898	899	900
901	902	903	904	905	906	907	908	909	910

Fill in.

525	526	527	528	529	530	531	532	533

	782	783	784	785	786	787	788	789	790

352	351	350	349	348	347	346	345	344

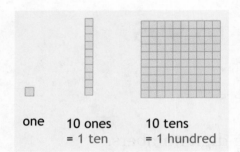

one	10 ones = 1 ten	10 tens = 1 hundred

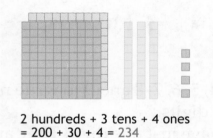

2 hundreds + 3 tens + 4 ones = 200 + 30 + 4 = 234

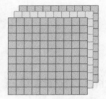

3 hundreds + 0 tens + 2 ones = 300 + 0 + 2 = 302

Exercise 1B

Write the numbers.

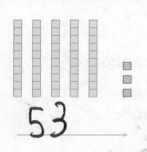

53

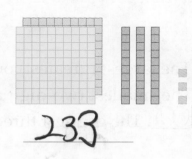

233

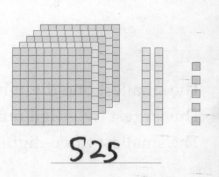

525

Fill in.

853 = **8** hundreds + **5** tens + **3** ones

362 = **3** hundreds + **6** tens + **2** ones

108 = **1** hundreds + **0** tens + **8** ones

420 = **4** hundreds + **2** tens + **0** ones

123 = **1** hundreds + **2** tens + **3** ones

75 = **0** hundreds + **7** tens + **5** ones

941 = **9** hundreds + **4** tens + **1** ones

638 = **6** hundreds + **3** tens + **8** ones

Write in the short form.

200 + 10 + 8 =	218
300 + 40 + 5 =	345
400 + 0 + 8 =	408
60 + 3 =	63
800 + 20 + 0 =	820

Write in the expanded form.

932 =	900 + 30 + 2
753 =	700 + 50 + 3
39 =	30 + 9
104 =	100 + 0 + 4
690 =	600 + 90 + 0

2

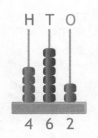

H T O

4 6 2

$462 = 4$ hundreds + 6 tens + 2 ones
$= 400 + 60 + 2$

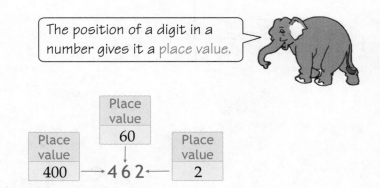

The position of a digit in a number gives it a place value.

	Place value
Place value	60
400	→ 4 6 2 ←

| Place value |
| 2 |

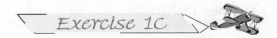

Exercise 1C

Fill in.

Number	Digit	Place value	Digit	Place value	Digit	Place value
276	2	200	7	70	6	6
672	6	600	7	70	2	2
726	6	6	7	700	2	20
67	6	60	7	7		
983	8	80	9	900	3	3
435	4	400	3	30	5	5
102	1	100	0	0	2	2

Write in words.

732 — seven hundred and thirty-two

158 — One hundred fifty eight

872 — eight hundred seventy

503 — five hendred three

246 — two hendred fortysix

663 — six hendred sixty three

777 — seven hundred seventy

463 — four hundred sixty three

601 — six hundred one

480 — four hundred eighty

737 — seven hundred thirty seven

946 — nine hundred fourty six

358 — three hundred fifty eight

860 — eight hundred sixty seven

3

98 99 100

Exercise 1D

Write the predecessor (the number before):

5**1** (52)   8**9** (90)   1**10** (111)   2**56** (257)   2**99** (300)

5**37** (538)   6**48** (649)   6**9** (70)   8**59** (860)   9**08** (909)

Write the successor (the number after):

(79) **80**   (169) **170**   (200) **201**   (352) **353**   (468) **469**

(307) **308**   (430) **431**   (729) **730**   (887) **888**   (945) **946**

Write the number between:

67 **68** 69   199 **200** 201   109 **110** 111   758 **759** 760   920 **921** 922

Continue the pattern.

| 472 | 476 | 480 | **484** | **488** | **492** | **496** |

| 540 | 560 | 580 | **600** | **620** | **640** | **660** |

| 950 | 900 | 850 | **800** | **750** | **700** | **650** |

To compare numbers, compare left to right. If the digits at a place are equal, compare the digits at the next place on the right.

H	T	O
	5	3

H	T	O
	5	3

T: 5 = 5   O: 3 = 3
53 = 53

H	T	O
4	2	7

H	T	O
5	0	2

H: 4 < 5
427 < 502

H	T	O
6	7	5

H	T	O
6	5	7

H: 6 = 6   T: 7 > 5
675 > 657

H	T	O
8	3	7

H	T	O
8	3	9

H: 8 = 8   T: 3 = 3   O: 7 < 9
837 < 839

H	T	O
1	6	3

H	T	O
	9	9

H: 1 > 0
163 > 99

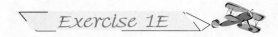
Exercise 1E

Write >, < or =.

721 > 45   83 > 49   76 < 97   7 < 13   89 < 98

703 > 356   98 < 389   145 > 45   467 > 439

876 > 786   371 = 371   256 < 562   316 > 306   714 > 114

438 = 438   533 < 583   975 > 957   666 < 999

Ring the smallest and tick the largest.

26	281	(15)	342✓	79	324

777✓	707	177	(17)	771	770

51	57	41	(29)	45	63✓

658	672✓	645	639	(619)	627

251	(132)	746	893✓	425	638

165	162	164	169✓	167	(161)

926✓	526	426	(26)	126	726

521	(125)	975✓	512	957	251

5

Write in ascending order (from the smallest to the largest).

40	20	10	60	80	50

10	20	40	50	60	80

23	15	72	65	38	44

15	23	38	44	65	72

458	851	589	578	854	815

458	578	589	815	851	854

653	685	635	658	697	679

635	653	658	679	685	697

902	920	29	92	290	209

29	92	209	290	902	920

Write in descending order (from the largest to the smallest).

438	519	284	209	290	765

765	519	438	290	284	209

356	275	194	419	653	527

653	527	419	356	275	194

489	894	733	337	373	984

984	894	733	373	337	489

652	526	715	749	480	634

749	715	652	634	526	480

129	902	328	497	664	504

902	664	504	497	328	129

$1+1=2$

Fill in.

In the week, _Thursday_ is the fifth day.

F is the sixth letter of the alphabet and _H_ is the eighth letter.

J is the _tenth_ letter of the alphabet and L is the _tewelfth_ letter.

In MATHEMATICS, H is the _fourth_ letter and C is the _tenth_ letter.

In WORKSHEETS, the letter T comes _at the end_ and H comes _at the end_

6

Do and Learn

Aim Making three-digit numbers

Things needed Cards numbered 0–9, sheets of paper, pencil

Do and Learn

1. Draw a table with three columns.
   Write hundreds, tens and ones, as shown.

2. Place a digit card in each column. Write down
   the number formed. Then change the places of
   the digits and write down the numbers formed.

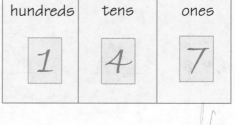

3. With 3 different digits (no zeros), you can make 6 three-digit numbers.
   For example, with 1, 4 and 7 you can make 147, 174, 417, 471, 741 and 714.
   Make three-digit numbers with some other digits.

When one digit is zero

4. Take the digits 5, 0 and 8.
   You cannot have 0 in the hundreds place because that gives a two-digit
   number. (058 is 58 and 085 is 85.)
   The three-digit numbers that you can make are 508, 580, 805 and 850.

Making the greatest number from three digits

5. Take the digits 4, 2 and 9.
   The greatest (largest) number will have the most
   hundreds and tens.
   So, arrange the digits in descending order, with
   the greatest digit at the hundreds place.
   The number is 942.

Making the smallest number from three digits

6. The smallest number formed with 4, 2 and 9 will have
   the least hundreds and tens.
   So, arrange the digits in ascending order, with the
   smallest digit at the hundreds place.
   The number formed is 249.

   What if one or more digits are zeros?
   Place them after the next-smallest digit.
   The smallest number with 0, 2 and 9 is 209.

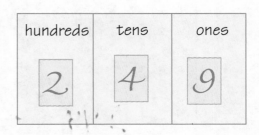

7

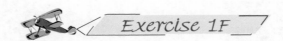

Make three-digit numbers using the given digits.

8, 2, 5	825	852	582	528	285	258
9, 3, 6	936	369	639	963	396	693
1, 7, 5	175	751	571	715	517	157
4, 9, 8	498	984	894	849	948	489
6, 4, 2	642	426	462	624	462	264
3, 6, 9	369	693	936	963	396	639

1, 0, 4	104	140	401	410	X	X
9, 5, 0	950	509	905	059	590	095
8, 2, 7	827	278	287	872	728	782
0, 4, 8	480	048	084	840	804	408

Make three-digit numbers and fill in.

Digits	Smallest number	Greatest number
8, 0, 6	608	860
7, 1, 5	157	751
6, 5, 2	256	652
9, 2, 4	249	924
5, 4, 0	045	540
6, 3, 9	369	963
0, 8, 9	089	980

Digits	Smallest number	Greatest number
4, 5, 0	045	540
9, 7, 8	789	987
3, 1, 6	136	631
0, 4, 2	024	420
5, 7, 6	567	765
8, 2, 4	248	842
3, 5, 4	345	543

2. Four-digit Numbers

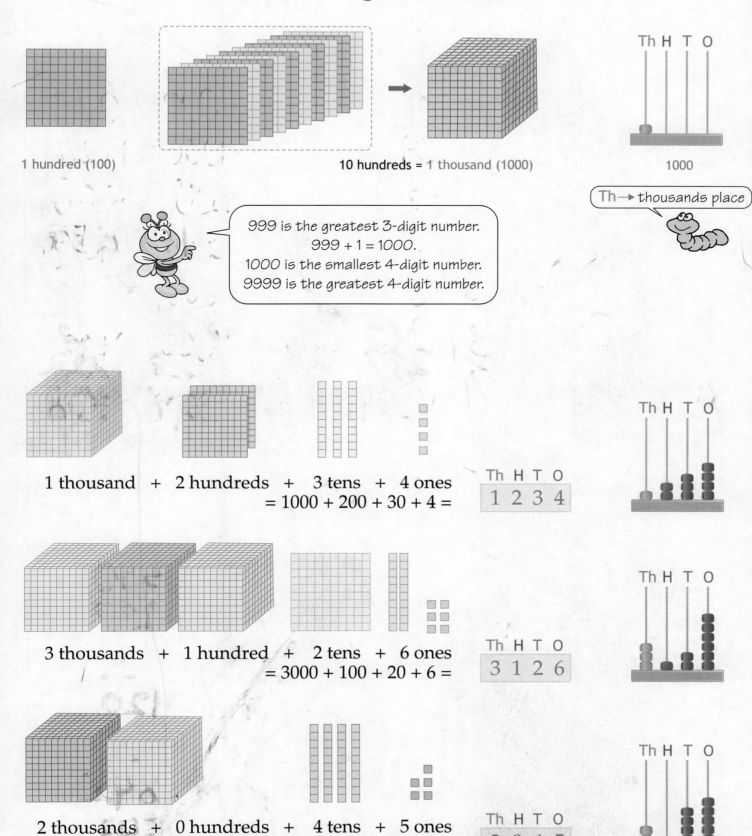

1 hundred (100)

10 hundreds = 1 thousand (1000)

1000

Th → thousands place

999 is the greatest 3-digit number.
999 + 1 = 1000.
1000 is the smallest 4-digit number.
9999 is the greatest 4-digit number.

1 thousand + 2 hundreds + 3 tens + 4 ones
= 1000 + 200 + 30 + 4 =

Th	H	T	O
1	2	3	4

3 thousands + 1 hundred + 2 tens + 6 ones
= 3000 + 100 + 20 + 6 =

Th	H	T	O
3	1	2	6

2 thousands + 0 hundreds + 4 tens + 5 ones
= 2000 + 0 + 40 + 5 =

Th	H	T	O
2	0	4	5

9

Fill in.

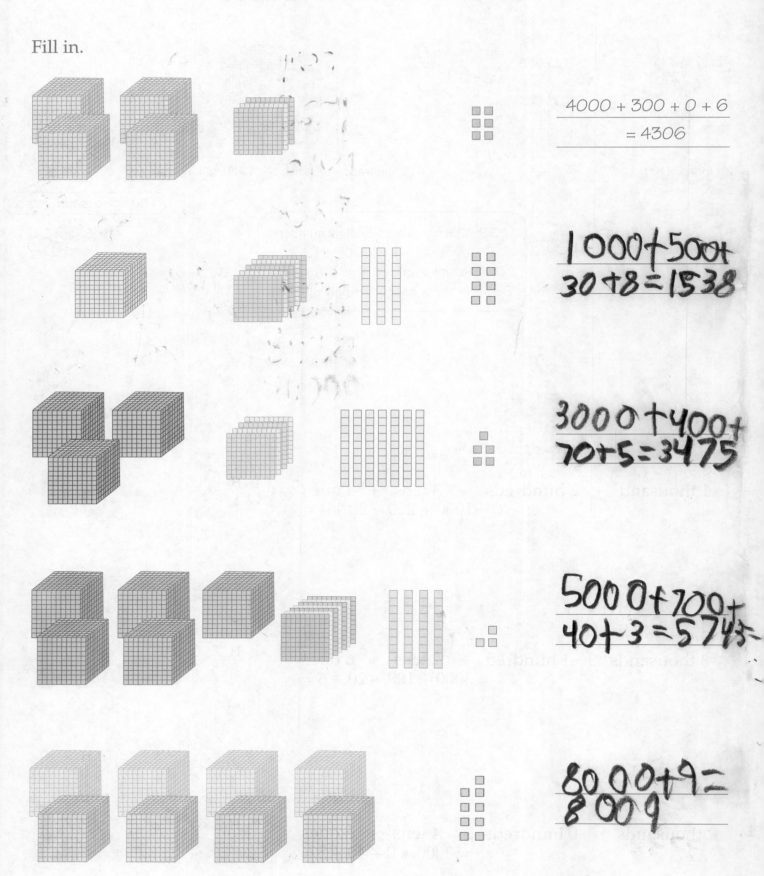

$4000 + 300 + 0 + 6$
$= 4306$

$1000 + 500 + 30 + 8 = 1538$

$3000 + 400 + 70 + 5 = 3475$

$5000 + 700 + 40 + 3 = 5743$

$8000 + 9 = 8009$

Fill in.

3 thousands + 4 hundreds + 6 tens + 4 ones = _3000 + 400 + 60 + 4_ = _3464_

1 thousand + 2 hundreds + 4 tens + 3 ones = 1000 + 200 + 40 + 3 = 1243

2 thousands + 3 hundreds + 7 tens + 5 ones = 2000 + 300 + 70 + 5 = 2375

3 thousands + 0 hundreds + 4 tens + 6 ones = 3000 + 0 + 40 + 6 = 3046

8 thousands + 6 hundreds + 5 tens + 0 ones = 8000 + 600 + 50 + 0 = 8650

7 thousands + 2 hundreds + 0 tens + 2 ones = 7000 + 200 + 0 + 2 = 7202

6 thousands + 5 hundreds + 4 tens + 3 ones = 6000 + 500 + 40 + 3 = 6543

2 thousands + 1 hundred + 2 tens + 5 ones = 2000 + 100 + 20 + 5 = 2125

4 thousands + 2 hundreds + 7 tens + 9 ones = 4000 + 200 + 70 + 9 = 4279

5 thousands + 3 hundreds + 8 tens + 1 one = 5000 + 300 + 80 + 1 = 5381

9 thousands + 9 hundreds + 9 tens + 9 ones = 9000 + 900 + 90 + 9 = 9999

Write the number shown on the abacus.

1223

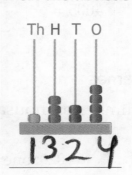
1324

3422

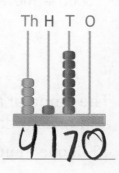
4170

3333

5307

7063

9592

11

Write in the short form.

2000 + 700 + 50 + 4 =	2754
1000 + 500 + 30 + 2 =	1532
3000 + 600 + 70 + 4 =	3674
5000 + 100 + 0 + 9 =	5109
4000 + 200 + 60 + 7 =	4267
6000 + 0 + 10 + 5 =	6015
9000 + 800 + 70 + 6 =	9876
8000 + 400 + 30 + 2 =	8432
7000 + 100 + 0 + 0 =	7100
2000 + 0 + 0 + 6 =	2006
3000 + 500 + 20 + 8 =	3528

Write in the expanded (long) form.

7304 =	7000 + 300 + 0 + 4
3268 =	3000 + 200 + 60 + 8
4769 =	4000 + 700 + 60 + 9
1024 =	1000 + 0 + 20 + 4
2836 =	2000 + 800 + 30 + 6
5417 =	5000 + 400 + 10 + 7
6642 =	6000 + 600 + 40 + 2
4598 =	4000 + 500 + 90 + 8
7364 =	7000 + 300 + 60 + 4
5810 =	5000 + 800 + 10
4005 =	4000 + 5

Number Names

The name of a four-digit number shows the number of thousands, hundreds, tens and ones it has.

1001: one thousand and one

1099: one thousand and ninety-nine

1115: one thousand one hundred and fifteen

2642: two thousand six hundred and forty-two

2726: two thousand seven hundred and twenty-six

3459: three thousand four hundred and fifty-nine

5934: five thousand nine hundred and thirty-four

7811: seven thousand eight hundred and eleven

8620: eight thousand six hundred and twenty

1020: one thousand and twenty

1100: one thousand one hundred

2500: two thousand five hundred

2066: two thousand and sixty-six

3004: three thousand and four

4052: four thousand and fifty-two

6013: six thousand and thirteen

8200: eight thousand two hundred

9090: nine thousand and ninety

Write the number names.

1326 = one thousand three hundred tewnty six

2578 = two thousand five nhundred t seventy eight

4729 = #our thousand seven hundred seventy eight

5017 = _____

6025 = _____

8054 = _____

3200 = _____

4700 = _____

9602 = _____

8309 = _____

1001 = _____

2007 = _____

3005 = _____

3850 = _____

Write in figures.

Three thousand eight hundred and fifty-four = _____

Six thousand nine hundred and forty-two = _____

Two thousand seven hundred and fifty = _____

Five thousand and sixty-three = _____

Eight thousand and one = _____

Seven thousand three hundred = _____

Three thousand nine hundred and six = _____

Write the number names.

2687 = _____

3651 = _____

9734 = _____

7308 = _____

5716 = _____

3007 = _____

4015 = _____

6200 = _____

8000 = _____

7069 = _____

5800 = _____

4530 = _____

6806 = _____

1254 = _____

2777 = _____

Write in figures.

Four thousand and seven = _____

Six thousand and forty-eight = _____

One thousand seven hundred = _____

Three thousand five hundred and four = _____

Nine thousand two hundred and fourteen = _____

Five thousand nine hundred and seventy eight = _____

Eight thousand six hundred and ninety-three = _____

Write the numbers that follow.

1005	1006	1007							
1250									
2325									
3467									
4893									
5295									
6732									
7888									

Count backwards and fill in the numbers.

1020	1019	1018					
1345							
3789							
4321							
6890							
8433							

Continue the pattern.

4000	4002	4004						
	5015	5020	5025					
1100	1200	1300						
	3500	3600	3700					

Fill in by counting forward.

3015 ☐ ☐ ☐ ☐ ☐ ☐ ☐ ☐ ☐

5792 ☐ ☐ ☐ ☐ ☐ ☐ ☐ ☐ ☐

6327 ☐ ☐ ☐ ☐ ☐ ☐ ☐ ☐ ☐

9010 ☐ ☐ ☐ ☐ ☐ ☐ ☐ ☐ ☐

7197 ☐ ☐ ☐ ☐ ☐ ☐ ☐ ☐ ☐

8888 ☐ ☐ ☐ ☐ ☐ ☐ ☐ ☐ ☐

5050 ☐ ☐ ☐ ☐ ☐ ☐ ☐ ☐ ☐

Count backwards and fill in.

2180 _____ _____ _____ _____ _____ _____ _____

4675 _____ _____ _____ _____ _____ _____ _____

5871 _____ _____ _____ _____ _____ _____ _____

9324 _____ _____ _____ _____ _____ _____ _____

7418 _____ _____ _____ _____ _____ _____ _____

Continue the pattern.

3020	3030	3040					
	2175	2170	2165				
1050	1100	1150					
	8590	8580	8570				
1111	1114	1117					
	5000	5011	5022				

Write the predecessor (the number before):

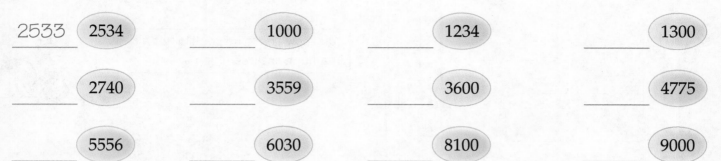

2533 (2534)   _____ (1000)   _____ (1234)   _____ (1300)

_____ (2740)   _____ (3559)   _____ (3600)   _____ (4775)

_____ (5556)   _____ (6030)   _____ (8100)   _____ (9000)

Write the successor (the number after):

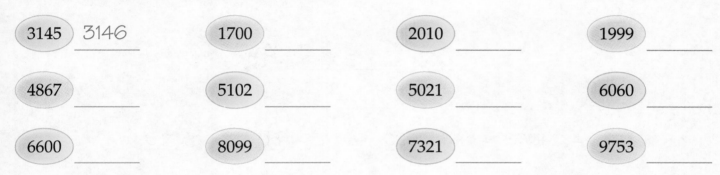

(3145) 3146   (1700) _____   (2010) _____   (1999) _____

(4867) _____   (5102) _____   (5021) _____   (6060) _____

(6600) _____   (8099) _____   (7321) _____   (9753) _____

Write the numbers before and after:

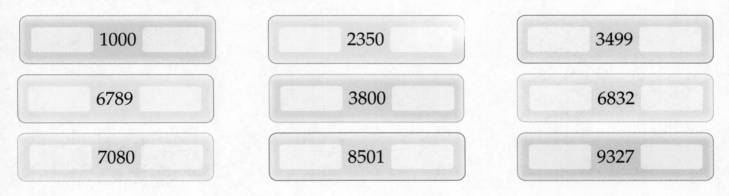

[ ] 1000 [ ]	[ ] 2350 [ ]	[ ] 3499 [ ]
[ ] 6789 [ ]	[ ] 3800 [ ]	[ ] 6832 [ ]
[ ] 7080 [ ]	[ ] 8501 [ ]	[ ] 9327 [ ]

Write the number beween:

6453 _6454_ 6455   999 _____ 1001   1110 _____ 1112   2345 _____ 2347

3897 _____ 3899   4998 _____ 5000   4030 _____ 4032   6814 _____ 6816

7877 _____ 7879   5309 _____ 5311   8099 _____ 8101   9835 _____ 9837

17

Place Values in Four-digit Numbers

Th H T O

5 1 2 3

$5123 = 5$ thousands $+ 1$ hundred $+ 2$ tens $+ 3$ ones
$\quad\quad = 5000 + 100 + 20 + 3$

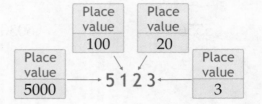

Place value 5000 → 5 1 2 3 ← Place value 3

Place value 100

Place value 20

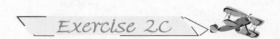

Exercise 2C

Write the place value of each digit.

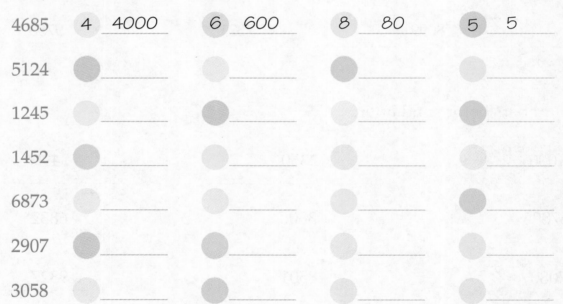

4685	4	4000	6	600	8	80	5	5
5124								
1245								
1452								
6873								
2907								
3058								

Fill in.

In 2458, 5 is in the _____ place, and 2 is in the _____ place.

In 7683, the digit in the thousands place is ___, and the place value of 8 is _____.

In 5714, the digit in the thousands place is ___, and its place value is _____.

In 4923, the place value of 9 is _____, that of 4 is _____ and that of 2 is _____ .

In 6039, the place value of 0 is _____, that of 9 is _____ and that of 6 is _____ .

Comparing and Arranging

To compare numbers, compare left to right.
If the digits at a place are equal, compare the digits at the next place on the right.

Th	H	T	O
4	2	3	5

Th	H	T	O
7	0	0	0

Th: 4 < 7
4235 < 7000

Th	H	T	O
1	2	3	4

Th	H	T	O
	9	9	9

Th: 1 > 0
1234 > 999

Th	H	T	O
9	8	7	6

Th	H	T	O
9	7	7	6

Th: 9 = 9   H: 8 > 7
9876 > 9776

Th	H	T	O
5	1	3	0

Th	H	T	O
5	1	4	5

Th: 5 = 5   H: 1 = 1   T: 3 < 4
5130 < 5145

Th	H	T	O
7	0	2	4

Th	H	T	O
7	0	2	4

Th: 7 = 7   H: 0 = 0   T: 2 = 2   O: 4 = 4
7024 = 7024

Exercise 2D

Write >, < or =.

2536 ◇ 3756   6622 ◇ 6262   999 ◇ 1025   2318 ◇ 54

7934 ◇ 9302   9000 ◇ 4000   6530 ◇ 6530   5378 ◇ 5368

8132 ◇ 8314   3924 ◇ 3920   1352 ◇ 1752   4534 ◇ 4354

9048 ◇ 9100   4678 ◇ 4678   5000 ◇ 4999   9235 ◇ 9325

Write the smallest number.

1023	1003	1002	1203	1302	*1002*
9456	3409	2278	997	6851	
6308	3409	2147	7326	5834	
5623	5326	5362	5632	5263	
4785	4875	4758	4857	4578	

Write the greatest number.

3467	3764	3647	3674	3746	*3764*
2893	1987	898	3680	4322	
7301	7031	7310	7103	7130	
5256	7428	8544	8600	6525	
6789	6978	6798	6897	6987	

Ring the smallest and tick the largest.

5789	(4327)	9328	5625	9723✓	4372

9834	9854	9852	9837	9821	9843

6584	6548	6458	6845	6485	6854

6200	6300	6020	6030	6099	6009

8503	2533	4438	2120	4847	6466

462	3518	5380	7634	1836	3759

Write in descending order (from the greatest to the smallest).

1100	890	2156	4329	1248	3736

4329, 3736, 2156, 1248, 1100, 890

1000	5000	7000	900	6000	8000

7328	3823	5548	4540	2389	6875

6582	8735	9821	7534	8573	6837

2548	2458	2854	2584	2485	2845

3076	760	3067	3760	3607	3670

Write in ascending order (from the smallest to the greatest).

3294	3924	3492	3942	3429	3249

3249, 3294, 3429, 3492, 3924, 3942

5000	2000	500	200	7000	700

5632	2411	3288	2388	3284	4365

8532	4729	7811	3502	5238	3333

2348	4328	4823	3248	2483	3842

1179	1719	1917	1197	1971	1791

Making the Smallest and the Greatest Numbers from Four Given Digits

Making the greatest number from four digits

The greatest number will have the most thousands, hundreds and tens. So, write the digits in descending order, with the greatest digit at the thousands place.

Given digits: 3, 1, 7, 5

Greatest number
with these digits: 7531

Given digits: 0, 9, 0, 6

Greatest number
with these digits: 9600

Making the smallest number from four digits

The smallest number will have the least thousands, hundreds and tens. So, write the digits in ascending order, with the smallest digit at the thousands place.
If there are zeros, place them after the next-smallest digit.
(You cannot have numbers starting with zeros.)

Given digits: 4, 2, 8, 6

Smallest number
with these digits: 2468

Given digits: 0, 2, 3, 0

Smallest number
with these digits: 2003

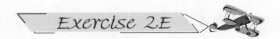
Exercise 2E

Make the greatest and the smallest four-digit numbers with the given digits.

Digits	Greatest number	Smallest Number
2, 6, 4, 4	6442	2446
3, 1, 7, 9		
5, 3, 4, 1		
8, 0, 7, 2		
1, 5, 2, 8		
7, 9, 4, 7		

Digits	Greatest number	Smallest Number
2, 9, 3, 7		
8, 4, 5, 6		
5, 1, 1, 9		
6, 0, 9, 8		
4, 0, 5, 0		
3, 4, 3, 3		

Some Numbers beyond 9999

What comes after 9999?

9999 + 1 = 10000 (ten thousand).

You know that 9 thousands together make 9,000.
Similarly, 10 thousands together make 10,000.
10,000 is the smallest five-digit number.

Here are some five-digit numbers.

A comma can separate the thousands digits. This helps in reading the number.

6740 → 6,740

45321 → 45,321

11,000	eleven thousand
15,000	fifteen thousand
19,300	nineteen thousand three hundred
16,452	sixteen thousand four hundred and fifty-two
20,000	twenty thousand
50,000	fifty thousand
35,681	thirty-five thousand six hundred and eighty-one
73,700	seventy-three thousand seven hundred
80,062	eighty thousand and sixty-two
99,999	ninety-nine thousand nine hundred and ninety-nine

99,999 is the greatest five-digit number.
What comes after 99,999?

99999 + 1 = 100000 (1 lakh **or** one hundred thousand).

100,000 is the smallest six-digit number.
100 thousands make 100,000.

Rewrite the numbers with commas and write their number names.

60342	60,342	sixty thousand three hundred and forty-two
10005		
16000		
25150		
42341		
70777		
81511		
96000		

3. Roman Numerals

We use numerals to write numbers. Usually, we use the numerals 0, 1, 2, 3, 4, 5, 6, 7, 8 and 9. But sometimes we use Roman numerals like I and V. You might have seen these on clock faces or on the sign outside a classroom. The Romans used seven letters as numerals. These numerals and their values are given below.

Roman numeral	I	V	X	L	C	D	M
Value	1	5	10	50	100	500	1000

To form numbers with these numerals, you have to follow certain rules.

- To form larger numbers, I, X, C and M can be repeated up to three times. The number formed is their sum.

  II = 1 + 1 = 2   III = 1 + 1 + 1 = 3   XX = 10 + 10 = 20

  CC = 100 + 100 = 200

  > Do not repeat V, L and D.

- A smaller numeral gets added to the greater numeral on its left.

  VI = 5 + 1 = 6   VII = 5 + 1 + 1 = 7   VIII = 5 + 1 + 1 + 1 = 8

  XI = 10 + 1 = 11   XV = 10 + 5 = 15   XXII = 10 + 10 + 1 + 1 = 22

- A smaller numeral gets subtracted from the greater numeral on its right.

  IV = 5 − 1 = 4   IX = 10 − 1 = 9   XL = 50 − 10 = 40

  > 4 is IV NOT IIII.

- A smaller numeral between two greater numerals gets subtracted from the numeral on its right.

  XIV = 10 + 5 − 1 = 14   XIX = 10 + 10 − 1 = 19

See how these rules are used in writing 1 to 20.

1	2	3	4	5	6	7	8	9	10	11	12	13	14	15	16	17	18	19	20
I	II	III	IV	V	VI	VII	VIII	IX	X	XI	XII	XIII	XIV	XV	XVI	XVII	XVIII	XIX	XX

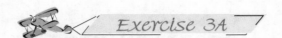

Exercise 3A

1. Write the numbers shown by the Roman numerals.

(a)

I	V	X	L	C	D	M

(b)

II	III	XX	XXX	CC	CCC

(c)

IV	IX	XIV	XIX	XXIV	XXIX

(d)

VI	VII	VIII	XI	XII	XIII	XVI	XXI	XXV

2. Write using Roman numerals.

(a)

3	4	1	2	9	10	11	15	13	16

(b)

7	5	8	14	18	19	12	6	17	20

3. Write 1 to 20 using Roman numerals.

4. Write the time.

2:00

Review Worksheet 1

1. Make the greatest and the smallest three-digit numbers with the given digits.

Digits	(a) 8, 3, 6	(b) 4, 3, 0	(c) 9, 5, 7
Smallest number			
Greatest number			

2. Write in the expanded form.

(a) 4672 =

(b) 6831 =

(c) 5015 =

(d) 9708 =

3. Write the numbers that follow.

(a) **1054** _____ _____ _____ _____ _____ _____

(b) **3646** _____ _____ _____ _____ _____ _____

(c) **8995** _____ _____ _____ _____ _____ _____

4. Write >, < or =.

(a) 4978 ⬦ 952   (b) 7807 ⬦ 7087   (c) 6534 ⬦ 6879   (d) 1274 ⬦ 2856

5. Write in descending order.

(a) | 5678 | 3251 | 6879 | 5231 | 6978 | _____

(b) | 9801 | 9108 | 8911 | 8091 | 8191 | _____

(c) | 6732 | 6237 | 6723 | 7632 | 7362 | _____

6. Fill in.

(a) In 3018, the place value of 8 is _____, that of 1 is _____ and that of 3 is _____.

(b) In 4852, the place value of 4 is _____, that of 5 is _____ and that of 8 is _____.

(c) Write the numbers shown by the numerals: XI = _____ IX = _____ VI = _____.

(d) Write in Roman numerals: 4 = _____   7 = _____   13 = _____.

4. Simple Addition and Subtraction

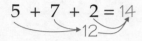

First let us go over things you know about addition.

5 + 7 + 2 = 14
→ 12 →

5 + 7 + 2 = 14
9

The sum of numbers in any order is the same.

number + 0 = same number

6 + 0 = 6   23 + 0 = 23
465 + 0 = 465   1378 + 0 = 1378

Addition of 10s, 100s and 1000s

10 + 10 = 20	20 + 10 = 30	40 + 10 = 50	70 + 10 = 80	90 + 10 = 100
100 + 100 = 200	300 + 100 = 400	500 + 100 = 600	700 + 100 = 800	800 + 100 = 900

1000 + 1000 = 2000   2000 + 1000 = 3000   3000 + 1000 = 4000   4000 + 1000 = 5000
5000 + 1000 = 6000   6000 + 1000 = 7000   7000 + 1000 = 8000   8000 + 1000 = 9000

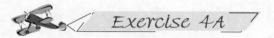

Exercise 4A

Add.

3 + 6 =	6 + 5 =	8 + 7 =	9 + 9 =
1 + 3 + 2 =	2 + 0 + 5 =	3 + 4 + 5 =	3 + 9 + 2 =
6 + 7 + 8 =	9 + 1 + 3 =	2 + 7 + 4 =	8 + 5 + 0 =
1 + 2 + 3 + 4 =	2 + 4 + 4 + 2 =	3 + 2 + 1 + 0 =	3 + 3 + 3 + 3 =
5 + 3 + 2 + 3 =	6 + 1 + 2 + 4 =	7 + 8 + 5 + 6 =	8 + 9 + 2 + 5 =

Expand and add.

25 + 43

20 + 5 + 40 + 3
= 20 + 40 + 5 + 3
= 60 + 8 = 68.

163 + 724

100 + 60 + 3 + 700 + 20 + 4
= 100 + 700 + 60 + 20 + 3 + 4
= 800 + 80 + 7 = 887.

Add 452 and 126.

4 5 2 + 1 2 6

4 hundreds + 5 tens + 2 ones
+ 1 hundred + 2 tens + 6 ones
= 5 hundreds + 7 tens + 8 ones = 578.

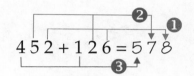

4 5 2 + 1 2 6 = 5 7 8

❶ Add the ones.
❷ Add the tens.
❸ Add the hundreds.

Exercise 4B

Expand and add.

23 + 74	321 + 45	460 + 37

251 + 134	524 + 333	603 + 295

Add.

32 + 46 = _____   44 + 21 = _____   72 + 16 = _____   269 + 30 = _____

145 + 23 = _____   27 + 421 = _____   343 + 142 = _____   264 + 534 = _____

186 + 610 = _____   675 + 312 = _____   541 + 347 = _____   716 + 152 = _____

Add.

```
  H T O
  3 5 4
+ 4 3 2
─────────
```
→
3 hundreds	and	5 tens	and	4 ones
+ 4 hundreds	and	3 tens	and	2 ones
7 hundreds	and	8 tens	and	6 ones
→
```
  H T O
  3 5 4
+ 4 3 2
─────────
  7 8 6
```

Add
❶ the ones, ❷ the tens,
❸ the hundreds.

Exercise 4C

Add.

```
  H T O          H T O          H T O          H T O          H T O
    1 2              4            3 2            5 5            6 6 7
+     7        + 1 9 2        +   4 6        +   2 1        +   2 2
─────────      ─────────      ─────────      ─────────      ─────────
```

```
    3 4            1 3 4          2 1 3          3 4 7          4 1 9
+ 3 2 3        + 2 6 2        + 5 4 6        + 5 3 2        + 3 8 0
─────────      ─────────      ─────────      ─────────      ─────────
```

```
  6 4 8          7 8 3          5 2 6          4 5 8          8 0 5
+ 1 4 1        + 2 0 5        + 3 6 2        + 2 0 0        + 1 8 4
─────────      ─────────      ─────────      ─────────      ─────────
```

Add.

```
  H T O          H T O          H T O          H T O          H T O
    1 7            1 0            7 2 6            4 5          2 3 6
+   3 0        +   8 6        +   5 0        + 6 0 3        + 1 6 2
─────────      ─────────      ─────────      ─────────      ─────────
```

```
  7 2 5          4 3 2          7 1 2          6 5 2          5 6 7
+ 2 5 4        + 4 3 2        + 2 5 6        + 3 4 7        + 3 2 1
─────────      ─────────      ─────────      ─────────      ─────────
```

Add.

	T	O
	3	1
+	2	5
+	2	2
	7	8

	T	O
	1	2
+	1	0
+	3	4

	T	O
	2	3
+	3	1
+	3	2

	T	O
	4	4
+	4	3
+	1	0

	T	O
	1	7
+	5	0
+	2	1

	6	2
+	2	3
+	1	4

	7	2
+	1	5
+	1	2

	3	3
+	1	2
+	2	1

	2	8
+	4	0
+	3	1

	5	4
+	2	3
+	2	0

	1	1
+	2	3
+	4	5

	6	3
+	1	2
+	1	3

	5	0
+	2	6
+	1	2

	4	5
+	2	2
+	3	0

	3	1
+	1	5
+	4	3

Add.

	H	T	O
	1	2	4
+	3	2	1
+	2	3	0
	6	7	5

	H	T	O
		3	1
+	4	3	4
+	3	1	3

	H	T	O
		4	3
+	1	4	4
+	5	1	0

	H	T	O
			4
+		2	3
+	8	5	2

	H	T	O
	7	0	2
+		1	5
+		8	1

	5	1	4
+	1	2	3
+		1	2

	4	2	0
+	2	4	0
+	1	2	0

	3	0	0
+	1	5	0
+	1	2	0

	5	7	3
+	1	2	5
+	2	0	1

	2	1	3
+	3	1	4
+	4	1	0

	3	1	6
+	2	6	1
+	2	1	2

	6	0	4
+	2	5	0
+	1	2	5

	1	3	2
+	4	3	2
+	3	1	2

	4	5	3
+	2	3	1
+	3	0	4

	6	3	3
+	1	2	4
+	2	3	1

Add.

1 + 2 + 3 + 4	4 + 5 + 6 + 7	2 + 3 + 11 + 21	6 + 2 + 20 + 50	3 + 4 + 21 + 61	2 + 4 + 40 + 32

63 + 12 + 12 + 2	52 + 13 + 4 + 20	35 + 12 + 11 + 30	40 + 24 + 13 + 21	34 + 30 + 21 + 12	52 + 14 + 21 + 1

24 + 13 + 20 + 11	34 + 23 + 12 + 20	40 + 16 + 21 + 12	33 + 20 + 30 + 14	2 + 11 + 12 + 53	44 + 22 + 10 + 12

Add.

4 + 32 + 420 + 340	2 + 13 + 522 + 260	250 + 4 + 32 + 403	311 + 100 + 244 + 123	221 + 321 + 222 + 135

302 + 214 + 152 + 130	200 + 210 + 220 + 230	521 + 250 + 117 + 111	431 + 203 + 153 + 101	312 + 154 + 120 + 212

Addition of Four-digit Numbers

Th	H	T	O
4	2	3	5
+ 2	6	5	2
6	8	8	7

⇌

+ 4 thousands and 2 hundreds and 3 tens and 5 ones
+ 2 thousands and 6 hundreds and 5 tens and 2 ones
6 thousands and 8 hundreds and 8 tens and 7 ones

Add
1 the ones,
2 the tens,
3 the hundreds,
4 the thousands.

Exercise 4D

Add.

Th	H	T	O
4	3	5	2
+	2	4	7

Th	H	T	O
7	6	4	5
+	1	3	0

Th	H	T	O
3	2	0	2
+ 4	6	5	1

Th	H	T	O
5	5	2	1
+ 3	2	4	3

3	5	4	2
+ 1	3	5	6

3	4	1	5
+ 5	4	7	1

6	9	4	8
+ 3	0	5	1

3	0	5	1
+ 6	9	4	8

4	3	2	1
+ 1	2	3	4

3	6	7	8
+ 6	2	1	0

2	4	5	8
+ 1	2	3	1

5	6	5	6
+ 4	1	3	2

Do these sums in your notebook.

3745 + 241	4657 + 340
4501 + 2377	7140 + 2852
5032 + 3865	4175 + 4712

31

Add.

Th	H	T	O
2	6	4	5
+ 1	0	2	3
+ 4	1	2	0
7	7	8	8

Th	H	T	O
6	3	2	0
+ 1	3	1	2
+	2	4	7

Th	H	T	O
4	3	4	3
+ 2	3	1	0
+	3	4	5

Th	H	T	O
8	0	2	4
+	5	3	1
+		2	2

5	4	0	3
+ 2	1	4	0
+ 1	4	2	5

6	1	3	2
+ 1	5	4	3
+ 2	2	1	4

4	2	3	1
+ 2	2	1	1
+ 1	4	5	3

3	1	0	2
+ 3	2	2	1
+ 2	3	6	6

Do these sums in your notebook.

4521 + 323 + 24

7427 + 1340 + 31

1234 + 1324 + 4320

5432 + 3210 + 1025

Add.

4	3	1	2
+ 1	2	2	1
+ 1	0	2	4
+ 2	3	1	0
8	8	6	7

8	2	3	1
+	4	3	2
+		2	3
+			2

4	2	4	2
+ 3	0	1	3
+ 1	1	2	2
+	6	2	1

3	1	2	3
+ 4	5	1	4
+ 1	3	3	0
+ 1	0	2	1

4	5	3	1
+ 1	0	3	2
+ 2	1	2	3
+ 1	2	0	2

6	5	4	3
+ 1	2	0	2
+ 1	0	1	2
+ 1	2	2	1

4	1	1	3
+ 1	3	4	2
+ 3	1	2	1
+ 1	2	1	1

5	0	0	0
+ 1	9	0	0
+ 2	0	9	0
+ 1	0	0	9

More sums = strong maths

Add.

```
  7 4 6 7
+     4 3 2
```

```
  9 2 5 3
+     6 0 4
```

```
  3 9 4 6
+ 5 0 3 2
```

```
  6 2 5 3
+ 1 5 3 4
```

```
  2 4 3 6
+ 2 5 3 2
```

```
  7 3 5 4
+ 1 2 3 5
```

```
  4 1 2 7
+ 3 6 5 0
```

```
  5 1 6 4
+ 3 6 2 3
```

```
  7 5 3 2
+   4 0 2
+     6 1
```

```
  4 0 3 1
+ 2 4 1 5
+ 1 2 3 2
```

```
  3 0 4 7
+ 2 6 2 1
+ 2 1 3 0
```

```
  6 0 2 1
+   8 4 2
+     2 0
+     1 3
```

```
  2 3 3 2
+ 3 0 3 4
+ 1 2 0 0
+ 1 3 1 2
```

Do these sums in your notebook.

5123 + 1640	6723 + 1142 +1031
7430 + 1545	5632 + 2101 + 1022
4533 + 2104	8712 + 143 + 12 + 1
2487 + 5312	2354 + 3131 + 1104 + 2310

33

A toy shop has 150 cars and 101 trains. It has 45 more dolls than the number of cars and trains together. How many dolls does the shop have?

$$\begin{array}{r} 150 \\ +\ 101 \\ +\ \ \ 45 \\ \hline 296 \end{array}$$

The shop has 296 dolls.

For the first show of a circus, 473 tickets were sold. For the second show, 525 tickets were sold. What was the total number of tickets sold?

A cobbler mended 23 shoes on Monday, 34 shoes on Tuesday and 22 shoes on Wednesday. How many shoes did he mend in all?

Minakshi is 7 years old. Her brother is 11 years old. Their mother's age is 21 years more than the sum of their ages. How old is their mother?

Do these sums in your notebook.

In a school, the girls planted 232 saplings. The boys planted 156 more saplings than the girls did. How many saplings did the boys plant?

Mr Ganesan bought 400 blue bulbs, 260 red bulbs and 125 yellow bulbs on Diwali. How many bulbs did he buy altogether?

A milk van was carrying 4235 packets of toned milk and 1260 packets of flavoured milk. How many packets was it carrying altogether?

A florist (flower seller) bought 1240 pink roses, 1135 yellow roses and 1510 white roses. How many roses did he buy in total?

34

Review of Subtraction

$7 - 0 = 7$ $26 - 0 = 26$ $891 - 0 = 891$ number – 0 = same number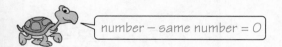

number – same number = 0 $4 - 4 = 0$ $53 - 53 = 0$ $637 - 637 = 0$

Subtraction of 10s, 100s and 1000s

$20 - 10 = 10$	$30 - 10 = 20$	$50 - 10 = 40$	$70 - 10 = 60$	$90 - 10 = 80$
$200 - 100 = 100$	$300 - 100 = 200$	$600 - 100 = 500$	$800 - 100 = 700$	$900 - 100 = 800$
$2000 - 1000 = 1000$	$3000 - 1000 = 2000$	$4000 - 1000 = 3000$	$5000 - 1000 = 4000$	
$6000 - 1000 = 5000$	$7000 - 1000 = 6000$	$8000 - 1000 = 7000$	$9000 - 1000 = 8000$	

Subtract.

```
  T O
  9 8
- 2 5
```
→
9 tens and 8 ones
– 2 tens and 5 ones
7 tens and 3 ones
→
```
  T O
  9 8
- 2 5
  7 3
```
→

❶
$98 - 25 = 73$
❷

Subtract.

```
H T O
7 4 3
-3 4 2
```
→
7 hundreds and 4 tens and 3 ones
– 3 hundreds and 4 tens and 2 ones
4 hundreds and 0 tens and 1 one
→
```
H T O
7 4 3
-3 4 2
4 0 1
```

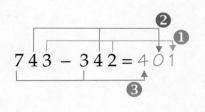

❷
❶
$743 - 342 = 401$
❸

Subtract
❶ the ones, ❷ the tens,
❸ the hundreds.

35

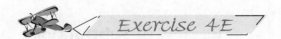

Exercise 4E

Subtract.

9 – 6 =	15 – 3 =	19 – 7 =	26 – 4 =
46 – 12 =	38 – 21 =	47 – 23 =	89 – 65 =
175 – 25 =	290 – 50 =	489 – 65 =	738 – 123 =
127 – 100 =	368 – 256 =	512 – 402 =	987 – 876 =

Subtract.

```
 H T O        H T O        H T O        H T O        H T O
   5 4          6 8          6 9        1 6 3        2 7 8
 -   3 2      -   2 3      -   5 4      -   5 2      -   7 5
```

```
   6 8 7        5 9 5        4 3 2        5 7 9        6 3 5
 -     4 6    -     6 2    -   3 2 1    -   5 2 3    -   5 3 2
 _____      _____      _____      _____      _____
```

```
   6 5 7        7 5 4        8 5 9        9 9 8        8 6 8
 - 4 3 3      - 5 2 3      - 6 2 4      - 7 0 6      - 3 2 3
```

Do these sums in your notebook.

46 – 26	598 – 47
285 – 144	647 – 346
796 – 451	836 – 503

36

Subtraction of Four-digit Numbers

```
Th H T O
  7 8 4 5        7 thousands and 8 hundreds and 4 tens and 5 ones
- 5 4 3 2      - 5 thousands and 4 hundreds and 3 tens and 2 ones
  2 4 1 3        2 thousands and 4 hundreds and 1 ten  and 3 ones
```

Subtract
1. the ones,
2. the tens,
3. the hundreds,
4. the thousands.

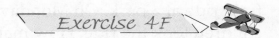

Exercise 4F

Subtract.

```
  1 4 5 7        2 8 3 9        6 7 8 5        2 5 1 8        2 8 7 6
-   4 3 2      -   6 0 4      -   2 7 3      - 1 5 0 1      - 2 2 2 1
```

```
  6 7 5 4        7 9 3 2        4 6 7 8        6 8 3 5        5 4 8 6
- 3 2 1 2      - 4 5 1 2      - 3 2 1 6      - 2 8 3 4      - 2 3 5 3
```

```
  9 8 8 6        5 2 1 4        6 8 4 2        9 9 9 9        7 9 8 5
- 7 2 3 5      - 3 2 1 4      - 3 4 2 1      - 8 7 6 5      - 3 6 3 2
```

Do these sums in your notebook.

2468 – 1234	8888 – 3210
7358 – 7358	8888 – 7654
6957 – 6425	7777 – 3456
8286 – 5250	6666 – 5432
9507 – 4203	5555 – 1234

Simi's mother is 31 years old. Her grandmother is 58 years old. What is the difference in age between them?

On Sunday, 57 children took the toy-train ride at a park. On Monday, 25 less children took the ride. How many took the ride on Monday?

India scored 124 runs more than Sri Lanka. If India scored 358 runs, how many runs did Sri Lanka score?

Of the 956 students in a school, 523 play football. How many do not play football?

Do these sums in your notebook.

By how much is 87 greater than 72?

By how much is 236 less than 496?

Armaan scored 6872 points in a game and Vivek scored 8994 points. What was the difference between their scores?

A baker has to bake 2850 cup cakes. If he has baked 1320 cakes, how many more does he have to bake?

Susan and Raj reached the finals of a music contest. Susan got 6278 votes and won by 155 votes. How many votes did Raj get?

MathGym

48 + 21 = 69 (sum)	125 + 243 = 368 (sum)
69 − 48 = 21	368 − 125 = 243
69 − 21 = 48	368 − 243 = 125

sum − one number = the other number

Fill in.

22	+	44	=	
52	+	37	=	
150	+	230	=	
324	+	432	=	

66	−		=	44
89	−		=	37
380	−		=	150
756	−		=	432

66	−		=	22
89	−		=	52
380	−		=	230
756	−		=	324

Fill in.

```
  6 2 4        7 ○ 3        2 ○ ○        5 3 ○        ○ 2 3        4 5 ○
+ 2 5 ○      + 2 1 4      + 3 4 2      + ○ 4 1      + 1 ○ 6      + 4 1 ○
─────        ─────        ─────        ─────        ─────        ─────
  8 7 8        9 7 7        5 9 2        7 7 3        9 9 9        8 6 0
```

Fill in.

50	+	30	=		+	60
15	+		=	12	+	16

34	+	42	=	36	+	
	+	31	=	22	+	34

81	+	18	=	80	+	
44	+		=	46	+	50

Fill in > or <.

I		II
VI		IV
VII		V
X		VII
XI		IX

V		IV
XI		X
III		IV
VIII		IX
X		IX

Match.

3 + 7	48 − 36
4 + 6 + 5	80 + 17
XII	X
24 + 35	95 − 80
91 + 6	33 + 26

Do and Learn

Aim To review regrouping

Things needed Sheets of squared paper from mathematics notebook, crayons, scissors

Do and Learn

1. Cut strips of squared paper. Each strip should have 10 squares.
   Colour two strips blue and the others pink.

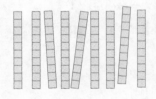

2. Cut squares from the blue strips. A blue square = 1. A pink strip = 10.

3. Cut square pieces that have 100 squares. Colour them green.
   A large green square = 100.
   You can 'exchange' a pink strip (10) for ten blue squares (1).
   You can also exchange a green square (100) for ten pink strips.

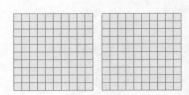

4. Show 2-digit or 3-digit numbers using the ones, tens and
   hundreds pieces. For example, you can show 215 as:

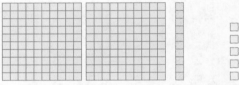

   215 = 2 hundreds + 1 ten + 5 ones

5. You can regroup by changing a hundred to 10 tens.
   Sometimes while subtracting we borrow a ten, hundred or
   thousand by regrouping like this.

   215 = 1 hundred + 11 tens + 5 ones

6. The number 420 can be shown as:

   420 = 3 hundreds + 12 tens + 0 ones

7. You can regroup by changing 10 tens
   to one hundred. We sometimes have
   to carry a ten, hundred or thousand
   while adding. We do it by regrouping.

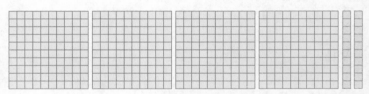

   420 = 4 hundreds + 2 tens + 0 ones

8. Show how the numbers 123, 345 and 627 can be shown in different ways by regrouping.

5. Addition with Carrying

Carrying Tens

Add 1235 and 426.

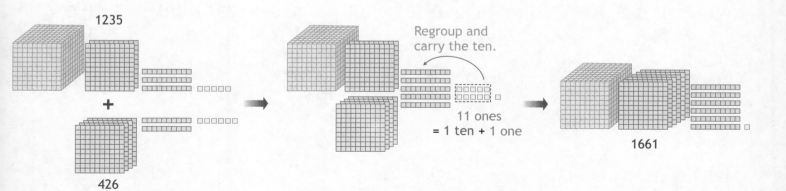

```
Th  H  T  O
         1
   1  2  3  5
+     4  2  6
─────────────
            1
```

O: 6 + 5 = 11
11 ones = 1 ten + 1 one.
Write 1 under O.
Carry 1 ten to T.

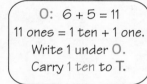

```
Th  H  T  O
         1
   1  2  3  5
+     4  2  6
─────────────
   1  6  6  1
```

T: 1 + 3 + 2 = 6
H: 2 + 4 = 6
Th: 1 + 0 = 1

Exercise 5A

Add.

1. (a)
```
    5 9
+   1 6
───────
```

(b)
```
    3 4
+   5 7
───────
```

(c)
```
    2 8
+   3 7
───────
```

(d)
```
  3 2 8
+   3 3
───────
```

(e)
```
  1 3 6
+   2 9
───────
```

(f)
```
  1 2 8
+ 1 2 8
───────
```

(g)
```
  6 0 2
+ 2 0 8
───────
```

(h)
```
  7 3 9
+ 2 2 4
───────
```

(i)
```
  5 3 6
+ 4 5 7
───────
```

(j)
```
  8 4 7
+ 1 3 5
───────
```

2.(a)
```
   7 3 2 9
+    5 3 8
_____
```

(b)
```
   2 3 2 6
+    4 5 4
_____
```

(c)
```
   3 6 1 8
+    1 5 9
_____
```

(d)
```
   6 3 2 7
+    4 1 6
_____
```

(e)
```
  1 0 3 8
+ 5 4 3 3
_____
```

(f)
```
  4 2 0 5
+ 3 1 3 7
_____
```

(g)
```
  5 6 8 7
+ 1 2 0 7
_____
```

(h)
```
  7 4 2 6
+ 1 3 5 9
_____
```

3.(a)
```
   4²8
+  2 8
+  1 5
_____
   9 1
```

(b)
```
   1 4
+  1 5
+  1 7
_____
```

(c)
```
   1 5
+  2 5
+  3 5
_____
```

(d)
```
   3 6
+  2 9
+  1 7
_____
```

(e)
```
   4 7
+  1 7
+  2 8
_____
```

4.(a)
```
  2 0 4
+ 1 5 2
+   1 6
_____
```

(b)
```
  1 0 8
+ 2 3 5
+ 3 2 2
_____
```

(c)
```
  3 5 6
+ 1 2 3
+ 4 1 6
_____
```

(d)
```
  5 2 5
+ 1 3 8
+ 2 1 7
_____
```

(e)
```
  4 2 7
+ 2 3 9
+ 3 1 6
_____
```

5.(a)
```
  1 3 2 2
+ 1 2 3 5
+ 4 1 2 3
_____
```

(b)
```
  2 4 1 4
+ 2 1 5 8
+ 3 3 0 2
_____
```

(c)
```
  3 1 3 6
+ 1 3 2 6
+ 4 5 0 6
_____
```

(d)
```
  4 1 3 5
+ 3 4 2 7
+   3 2 0
_____
```

(e)
```
  5 5 4 8
+ 2 3 0 5
+ 1 0 2 7
_____
```

(f)
```
  6 3 0 7
+ 1 2 2 6
+ 1 3 4 9
_____
```

(g)
```
  4 2 1 0
+ 2 3 4 8
+ 2 4 1 9
_____
```

(h)
```
  6 5 3 9
+   1 2 7
+   2 2 9
_____
```

6. (a)
```
    4 2
+   1 4
+   2 2
+     3
```

(b)
```
    2 5
+   3 3
+   1 4
+   2 1
```

(c)
```
    3 1
+   1 2
+   2 6
+   1 4
```

(d)
```
    2 5
+   2 5
+   2 5
+   1 5
```

(e)
```
    1 7
+   1 8
+   1 9
+   2 0
```

7. (a)
```
  2 3 2
+ 2 2 2
+ 3 0 3
+   1 4
```

(b)
```
  3 1 2
+ 1 2 3
+ 3 0 4
+ 1 4 5
```

(c)
```
  1 4 4
+ 1 1 6
+ 2 1 5
+ 3 1 1
```

(d)
```
  2 1 5
+ 1 2 6
+ 2 3 7
+ 1 1 2
```

(e)
```
  3 3 6
+ 2 0 5
+ 1 2 3
+ 1 1 8
```

8. (a)
```
  1 3 2 1
+ 1 0 3 5
+ 1 2 1 6
+ 1 1 1 3
```

(b)
```
  5 4 2 4
+ 2 1 1 4
+ 1 2 2 4
+ 1 2 1 4
```

(c)
```
  4 2 3 7
+ 1 1 0 2
+ 2 0 2 7
+ 1 4 1 7
```

(d)
```
  6 1 0 6
+ 1 2 0 5
+ 1 3 0 7
+ 1 1 4 4
```

Carrying Hundreds

Th	H	T	O
		1	
	3	4	5	2
+	4	3	7	4
	7	8	2	6

O: 4 + 2 = 6
T: 5 + 7 = 12
   12 tens = 10 tens + 2 tens = 1 hundred + 2 tens.
   Write 2, carry 1 hundred.
H: 1 + 4 + 3 = 8   Th: 3 + 4 = 7

```
  1
    4 7
+   8 1
  1 2 8
```

```
    1 1
  2 5 6 5
+ 1 2 4 5
  3 8 1 0
```

```
    2 2
  4 0 5 7
+ 1 2 8 7
+ 1 3 7 9
  6 7 2 3
```

43

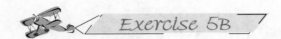

Do these sums.

1. (a)
```
    5 3
+ 7 4
```

(b)
```
    2 5
+ 8 2
```

(c)
```
    5 6
+ 7 3
```

(d)
```
    9 3
+ 4 8
```

(e)
```
  3 6 6
+    3 6
```

(f)
```
  4 5 7
+    8 7
```

(g)
```
  3 5 1
+ 4 9 6
```

(h)
```
  2 5 6
+ 2 5 6
```

(i)
```
  6 7 5
+ 1 4 9
```

(j)
```
  5 6 9
+ 2 3 1
```

2. (a)
```
  6 3 5 4
+        6 4
```

(b)
```
  4 6 3 8
+     1 6 2
```

(c)
```
  5 5 4 1
+ 2 1 9 3
```

(d)
```
  7 3 8 9
+ 1 2 4 6
```

(e)
```
  5 8 3 7
+ 3 0 7 6
```

(f)
```
  1 2 7 4
+ 2 1 8 6
```

(g)
```
  3 1 6 2
+ 4 4 6 9
```

(h)
```
  4 3 9 8
+ 5 2 9 8
```

3. (a)
```
    5 3
+ 7 2
+    4
```

(b)
```
    4 1
+ 5 2
+ 6 3
```

(c)
```
    6 3
+ 5 1
+ 9 2
```

(d)
```
    2 3
+ 6 7
+ 3 2
```

(e)
```
  1 6 4
+    5 3
+    7 4
```

(f)
```
  3 6 7
+ 1 8 7
+    8 7
```

(g)
```
  1 5 3
+ 1 4 7
+ 1 7 6
```

(h)
```
  4 6 5
+ 3 8 5
+ 1 3 5
```

(i)
```
  3 6 8
+ 2 5 6
+ 1 9 7
```

(j)
```
  5 9 4
+ 1 4 9
+ 1 5 7
```

4. (a)
```
   3 1 2 0
 +   3 5 4
 +     6 5
```

(b)
```
   2 1 7 4
 + 1 3 6 2
 +   4 3 5
```

(c)
```
   7 0 7 1
 + 1 4 5 9
 +   3 8 6
```

(d)
```
   6 5 1 4
 + 2 1 8 5
 + 1 0 9 0
```

(e)
```
   4 3 5 6
 + 1 2 7 4
 + 2 1 9 5
```

(f)
```
   3 0 6 7
 + 2 3 7 6
 + 2 1 3 7
```

(g)
```
   2 1 8 3
 + 4 2 7 9
 + 2 3 5 8
```

(h)
```
   2 1 6 8
 + 3 2 8 8
 + 4 1 6 8
```

5. (a)
```
   3 1
 + 7 0
 + 1 2
 +   4
```

(b)
```
   3 2
 + 4 2
 + 5 2
 + 6 2
```

(c)
```
   1 3
 + 2 3
 + 3 3
 + 4 3
```

(d)
```
   2 6
 + 3 3
 + 4 4
 + 4 1
```

(e)
```
   4 9
 + 3 2
 + 2 7
 + 3 3
```

6. (a)
```
   1 3 1
 + 1 5 2
 +   1 3
 +   1 0
```

(b)
```
   4 5 3
 + 2 4 4
 +   6 3
 +   7 8
```

(c)
```
   1 3 8
 + 2 5 4
 + 1 4 4
 + 2 6 8
```

(d)
```
   3 1 2
 + 1 4 5
 + 2 7 7
 + 1 9 2
```

(e)
```
   2 4 5
 + 2 5 6
 + 1 6 7
 + 1 5 8
```

7. (a)
```
   1 4 5 3
 +   2 3 1
 +     4 2
 +       1
```

(b)
```
   4 2 7 8
 + 1 3 6 4
 +   1 2 3
 +     7 2
```

(c)
```
   2 3 5 6
 + 1 0 7 3
 + 2 1 8 4
 + 1 2 4 7
```

(d)
```
   1 1 9 9
 + 2 2 3 4
 + 3 3 5 6
 + 1 0 5 2
```

Carrying Thousands

```
  Th H T O
   1
   3 6 2 5
 + 3 8 4 1
 ─────────
   7 4 6 6
```

O: 5 + 1 = 6   T: 2 + 4 = 6
H: 6 + 8 = 14
    14 hundreds = 10 hundreds + 4 hundreds
               = 1 thousand + 4 hundreds.
    Write 4, carry 1 thousand.
Th: 1 + 3 + 3 = 7

```
   1
     4 3 5
   + 7 2 3
   ───────
   1 1 5 8
```

```
   1 1 1
   4 7 2 9
 + 2 4 8 3
 ─────────
   7 2 1 2
```

```
   2     1
   3 7 2 6
 + 1 9 0 1
 +   5 3 7
 ─────────
   6 1 6 4
```

Exercise 5C

Add.

1. (a)
```
   5 7 2
 + 6 2 4
```
(b)
```
   2 3 5
 + 8 0 8
```
(c)
```
   4 6 5
 + 5 9 2
```
(d)
```
   2 8 7
 + 9 3 6
```
(e)
```
   8 4 7
 + 7 6 9
```

2. (a)
```
   1 4 5 3
 +   7 2 4
```
(b)
```
   2 5 7 8
 +   4 7 1
```
(c)
```
   3 5 1 2
 +   5 8 9
```
(d)
```
   4 6 8 3
 +   6 5 8
```

(e)
```
   1 5 5 6
 + 2 6 4 3
```
(f)
```
   2 4 7 9
 + 3 9 4 0
```
(g)
```
   3 7 6 8
 + 4 2 3 2
```
(h)
```
   5 6 6 6
 + 2 4 5 6
```

3. (a)
```
   4 1 2
 + 5 0 3
 + 6 6 4
```
(b)
```
   5 3 4
 + 7 2 5
 + 2 3 3
```
(c)
```
   4 7 8
 + 1 5 6
 + 8 2 1
```
(d)
```
   7 3 9
 + 8 8 9
 + 4 1 2
```
(e)
```
   6 6 3
 + 9 7 3
 + 8 6 5
```

4. (a)
```
   4 5 1 4
 + 2 4 1 2
 + 1 3 2 3
   8 2 4 9
```
(b)
```
   2 5 7 9
 + 2 6 6 0
 + 2 3 2 3
```
(c)
```
   3 4 8 6
 + 2 7 8 6
 + 2 9 8 6
```
(d)
```
   1 5 3 5
 + 3 9 6 7
 + 2 6 9 8
```

5. (a)
```
   5 5 5
 + 6 3 2
 + 3 0 1
 +   1 1
```
(b)
```
   1 5 2
 + 3 1 4
 + 7 6 3
 + 1 4 5
```
(c)
```
   2 5 3
 + 4 2 3
 + 5 3 3
 + 3 4 3
```
(d)
```
   2 4 6
 + 7 4 7
 + 8 4 5
 + 4 4 3
```
(e)
```
   4 8 5
 + 6 8 5
 + 7 4 3
 + 3 1 4
```

6. (a)
```
   5 6 2 3
 + 3 4 1 2
 +     2 0
 +       3
```
(b)
```
   2 5 3 4
 + 1 4 7 2
 + 2 1 3 3
 + 2 3 1 3
```
(c)
```
   2 5 3 2
 + 3 5 4 1
 + 1 5 2 4
 + 1 5 3 6
```
(d)
```
   2 6 3 5
 + 1 4 5 6
 + 2 5 4 3
 + 1 6 6 7
```

7. Do these sums in your notebook.

(a) 58 + 27 (b) 26 + 46 (c) 63 + 48 (d) 46 + 87 (e) 35 + 99

(f) 429 + 23 (g) 450 + 450 (h) 274 + 567 (i) 645 + 848 (j) 939 + 91

(k) 1267 + 35 (l) 1557 + 346 (m) 4182 + 1649 (n) 3271 + 1873 (o) 3273 + 57

(p) 264 + 3558 (q) 4572 + 543 (r) 7376 + 1646 (s) 3245 + 1987 (t) 25 + 8975

(u) 12 + 25 + 36 (v) 32 + 64 + 578 (w) 250 + 168 + 239 (x) 2875 + 1624 + 1532

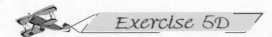

1. Srikanth scored 85 marks in English, 87 marks in science and 92 marks in maths. Find his total marks.

2.  A library has 178 more fairy-tale books than comics. If it has 396 comics, how many fairy-tale books does it have?

3. A shop has 3575 DVDs of Hindi films and 3455 DVDs of English films. How many DVDs does it have altogether?

4.  A restaurant needs to serve sambar, rasam and chutney in separate bowls to 115 guests. How many bowls are needed?

5. Do these sums in your notebook.

(a) My grandfather is 26 years older than my father. My father is 28 years older than me. I am 9 years old. How old is my grandfather?

(b) There are 3346 men, 3145 women and 2985 children in a small town. What is the population (total number of people) of the town?

(c) A store house has 2468 bottles of apple juice, 3134 bottles of orange juice and 1452 bottles of grape juice. How many bottles of juice does it have?

(d) The visitors at a fair on the first two days were 1457 and 2357. On the third day, there were 1200 more visitors than the visitors on the first two days taken together. How many people visited the fair on the third day?

6. Subtraction with Borrowing

Borrowing Tens

Subtract 1129 from 2241.

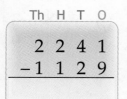

O: 1 – 9 ✗
So, regroup in 2241 and subtract.

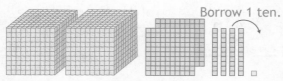

2 thousands + 2 hundreds + 4 tens + **1 one**
2241

Borrow 1 ten.

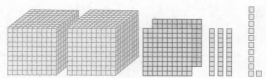

2 thousands + **2 hundreds** + 3 tens + **11 ones**
2241

```
   Th H T O
          3 11
    2 2 4̶ 1̶
  – 1 1 2 9
  ─────────
    1 1 1 2
```

Rewrite 4 tens and 1 one as 3 tens and 11 ones. Then subtract.

Exercise 6A

Subtract.

1. (a)
```
    2 6
  –   8
  ─────
```
(b)
```
    4 8
  –   9
  ─────
```
(c)
```
    3 5
  – 1 7
  ─────
```
(d)
```
    4 2
  – 2 8
  ─────
```
(e)
```
    5 0
  – 3 7
  ─────
```

(f)
```
    4 0
  – 1 5
  ─────
```
(g)
```
    5 6
  – 3 8
  ─────
```
(h)
```
    6 4
  – 4 7
  ─────
```
(i)
```
    7 3
  – 5 4
  ─────
```
(j)
```
    9 8
  – 8 9
  ─────
```

2. (a)
```
  1 3 4
-   2 7
```

(b)
```
  4 7 5
-   5 6
```

(c)
```
  2 2 4
- 1 1 6
```

(d)
```
  3 7 8
- 1 4 9
```

(e)
```
  5 7 0
- 5 2 3
```

(f)
```
  6 8 5
- 4 3 7
```

(g)
```
  7 5 4
- 5 2 8
```

(h)
```
  8 7 1
- 8 1 8
```

(i)
```
  9 8 0
- 4 0 6
```

(j)
```
  8 6 3
- 3 2 9
```

3. (a)
```
  2 6 7 5
-   4 3 8
```

(b)
```
  1 5 4 0
-   2 3 7
```

(c)
```
  3 4 6 2
-   3 4 6
```

(d)
```
  5 5 5 5
-   5 2 6
```

(e)
```
  6 0 9 5
- 6 0 7 9
```

(f)
```
  7 9 9 4
- 4 0 3 7
```

(g)
```
  8 6 6 7
- 8 6 3 9
```

(h)
```
  9 3 2 3
- 8 3 0 5
```

Borrowing Tens and Hundreds

Th H T O
```
      4  12
  4  5̶  2̶  7
- 2  3  7  5
  ‾‾‾‾‾‾‾‾‾‾
  2  1  5  2
```

O: 7 – 5 = 2   T: 2 – 7 ✗
In 4527, there are 5 hundreds.
Borrow 1 hundred, regrouping
to 4 hundreds and 12 tens.
Then T: 12 – 7   H: 4 – 3

O: 2 – 6 ✗
But 8612 = 8000 + 600 + 1 ten + 2 ones.
Borrow 1 ten and regroup to 0 tens and 12 ones.
Then O: 12 – 6 = 6   T: 0 – 7

T: 0 – 7 ✗   Borrow 1 hundred, regrouping
to 5 hundreds and 10 tens.
Then T: 10 – 7   H: 5 – 3

Th H T O
```
         5  10
         6̶  1̶  12
  8  6  1  2̶
- 5  3  7  6
  ‾‾‾‾‾‾‾‾‾‾
  3  2  3  6
```

50

```
 Th  H  T  O                                              Th  H  T  O
        3  10                                                    9  10
                                                             3  10
    9  4̶  0̶  0                                            9  4̶  0̶  0̶
  −    2  8  5                                          −    2  8  5
                                                          9  1  1  5
```

O: We need to borrow 1 ten.
9400 has 0 tens, but 4 hundreds.
Borrow 1 hundred (= 10 tens).
Then H: 3 − 2   T: 10 − 8

Now borrow 1 ten.
Then T: 9 − 8
        O: 10 − 5

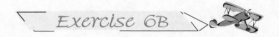

Exercise 6B

Subtract.

1. (a)
```
    5 2 8
  −   3 7
```
(b)
```
    1 4 6
  −   5 6
```
(c)
```
    4 0 7
  −   2 3
```
(d)
```
    5 2 8
  − 2 8 6
```
(e)
```
    6 3 4
  − 4 6 8
```

(f)
```
    7 3 5
  − 1 4 9
```
(g)
```
    6 5 0
  − 2 7 9
```
(h)
```
    7 0 3
  − 6 4 5
```
(i)
```
    9 0 0
  − 2 4 6
```
(j)
```
    4 4 2
  − 3 6 7
```

2. (a)
```
    4 3 2 8
  −     3 6
```
(b)
```
    2 6 9 7
  −   2 9 8
```
(c)
```
    3 7 3 9
  − 1 4 4 9
```
(d)
```
    5 9 1 3
  − 2 7 8 5
```

(e)
```
    7 6 8 4
  −   3 8 5
```
(f)
```
    5 8 0 0
  −   2 4 3
```
(g)
```
    6 1 0 3
  − 4 0 3 7
```
(h)
```
    8 5 5 7
  − 8 4 9 9
```

3. Do these sums in your notebook.

(a) 265 − 93   (b) 543 − 72   (c) 681 − 85   (d) 704 − 56

(e) 248 − 184   (f) 470 − 365   (g) 510 − 231   (h) 806 − 759

(i) 2543 − 67   (j) 4914 − 3826   (k) 8300 − 7235   (l) 5621 − 5537

Borrowing Tens, Hundreds and Thousands

	Th	H	T	O
	6	13		
	7̶	3̶	6	4
−	5	5	3	4
	1	8	3	0

O: 4 − 4 = 0   T: 6 − 3 = 3
H: 3 − 5 ✗
In 7364, there are 7 thousands.
Borrow 1 thousand (= 10 hundreds).
Then Th: 6 − 5   H: 13 − 5

	Th	H	T	O
	4	10		
	5̶	0̶	0	1
−	2	1	7	5

O: We need to borrow 1 ten.
But 5001 = 5000 + 0 + 0 + 1
So regroup. First borrow
1 thousand (10 hundreds).
Then Th: 4 − 2   H: 10 − 1

	Th	H	T	O
		9	9	11
	4	1̶0̶	1̶0̶	
	5̶	0̶	0̶	1
−	2	1	7	5
	2	8	2	6

Borrow 1 hundred (10 tens).
Then H: 9 − 1   T: 10 − 7
Borrow 1 ten (10 ones).
Then T: 9 − 7   O: 11 − 5

Exercise 6C

Subtract.

1.(a)
```
    5 3 4 5
  −   6 2 3
```

(b)
```
    4 4 5 9
  −   7 9 8
```

(c)
```
    3 5 3 8
  − 1 6 2 1
```

(d)
```
    7 6 4 5
  − 3 8 5 5
```

(e)
```
    2 7 5 6
  − 1 8 6 2
```

(f)
```
    5 4 6 2
  − 3 5 9 6
```

(g)
```
    4 2 3 5
  − 2 7 4 7
```

(h)
```
    6 4 1 2
  − 3 2 6 4
```

(i)
```
    9 1 2 3
  − 5 3 7 6
```

(j)
```
    7 0 5 6
  − 5 1 4 7
```

(k)
```
    4 0 0 4
  − 2 5 6 9
```

(l)
```
    5 0 0 0
  − 3 2 4 5
```

2. Do these sums in your notebook.

(a) 1586 − 655   (b) 2714 − 846   (c) 4319 − 2843   (d) 7235 − 4658   (e) 9114 − 8647

Practice = strong maths

Exercise 6D

Subtract.

1. (a)
```
  9 1
-   7
```
(b)
```
  8 4
-   6
```
(c)
```
  7 8
- 6 8
```
(d)
```
  5 6
- 2 8
```
(e)
```
  6 0
- 4 4
```

2. (a)
```
  2 6 3
-   4 5
```
(b)
```
  3 7 2
-   8 6
```
(c)
```
  4 1 5
- 2 6 7
```
(d)
```
  6 0 0
- 4 3 8
```
(e)
```
  8 0 1
- 5 7 4
```

(f)
```
  6 3 8
- 3 2 9
```
(g)
```
  7 1 1
- 4 1 4
```
(h)
```
  5 1 2
- 2 5 6
```
(i)
```
  7 0 0
- 3 5 0
```
(j)
```
  9 7 2
- 4 7 8
```

3. (a)
```
  2 5 6 7
-   3 5 8
```
(b)
```
  4 8 5 2
-   4 8 5
```
(c)
```
  6 2 2 6
-   2 3 7
```
(d)
```
  7 0 0 4
-   4 9 7
```

(e)
```
  1 3 5 7
- 1 2 7 8
```
(f)
```
  4 4 6 8
- 3 5 7 9
```
(g)
```
  6 0 1 0
- 4 2 3 1
```
(h)
```
  8 0 0 0
- 4 5 1 1
```

4. Do these sums in your notebook.

(a) 66 – 27   (b) 186 – 89   (c) 751 – 95   (d) 803 – 66

(e) 486 – 269   (f) 321 – 197   (g) 402 – 204   (h) 900 – 450

(i) 2743 – 54   (j) 3151 – 2163   (k) 8102 – 6204   (l) 7300 – 4562

Adding and Subtracting in Steps

Find 1456 – 2437 + 3147.

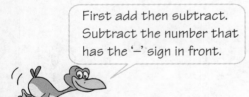

First add then subtract. Subtract the number that has the '–' sign in front.

❶
```
      1  1
   1  4  5  6
 + 3  1  4  7
 ───────────
   4  6  0  3
```

❷
```
         9  13
      5  10
   4  6  0  3
 − 2  4  3  7
 ───────────
   2  1  6  6   Answer
```

Find 7526 – 1932 – 2085.

❶
```
   6  14
   7  5  2  6
 − 1  9  3  2
 ───────────
   5  5  9  4
```

❷
```
         8  14
   5  5  9  4
 − 2  0  8  5
 ───────────
   3  5  0  9   Answer
```

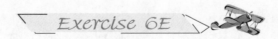

Exercise 6E

Do these sums in your notebook.

1. (a) 46 + 32 – 17   (b) 65 – 38 + 27   (c) 53 – 66 + 48   (d) 34 – 19 + 45

   (e) 24 – 12 – 11   (f) 96 – 58 – 14   (g) 89 – 23 – 18   (h) 56 – 28 – 28

2. (a) 359 + 83 – 247   (b) 575 – 453 + 618   (c) 285 – 546 + 638   (d) 623 – 215 – 116

   (e) 698 – 400 – 23   (f) 146 – 267 + 735   (g) 642 – 68 – 124   (h) 537 – 320 + 173

3. (a) 3124 – 2846 + 4649   (b) 1024 – 512 – 512   (c) 5283 – 6271 + 2345

   (d) 6200 – 1001 – 2781   (e) 4352 + 45 – 2967   (f) 1045 – 1725 + 8317

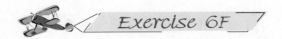

1. At a dog show there were 35 Alsatians. The number of pugs was 18 less. How many pugs were there at the show?

2.  Lisa's grandfather is 61 years old. Her aunt is 28 years younger than him. How old is her aunt?

3. Mr Barua ordered 925 cups of ice cream for his party. At the end of the party, 189 cups were left. How many cups of ice cream did the guests have?

4.  A poultry farm sold 5392 eggs in a week. It sold 1587 less eggs the next week. How many eggs did it sell the second week?

5. Do these sums in your notebook.

   (a) Super Express has 624 seats. 128 seats are in AC coaches. How many seats are there in non-AC coaches?

   (b) If 286 students join a school, the school will have 1500 students. How many students does the school have now?

   (c) There were 8725 people watching a match in a stadium. During a break, only 2658 people remained in the stadium. How many people went out?

   (d) What number when added to 500 gives 750?

   (e) What number when added to 4569 gives 7241?

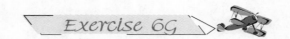

1. 350 children were going to Kerala. 135 children travelled by bus, 27 by car, and the rest took a train. How many travelled by train?

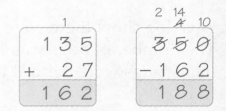

188 children travelled by train.

2. To decorate their Christmas trees, Joe bought 25 stars and 55 bulbs, and Ann bought 24 stars and 65 bulbs. Who bought more decoration items?

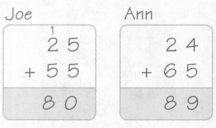

Ann bought more.

3. A wildlife park in India had 370 elephants. 25 of them were sent to Nepal and 7 were sent to Bangladesh. How many elephants were left in the park?

4. On 1 May, there were 1275 tourists in Mumbai. On 2 May, 983 more tourists came in, and 1163 left for Goa. How many tourists were there in Mumbai on 2 May?

5. Do these sums in your notebook.

(a) Anil had 64 colour pencils. He lost 35 of them. Then his mother bought him a box of 24 colour pencils. How many colour pencils does he have now?

(b) A shop sold 350 veggie burgers and 215 nonveg burgers on Sunday. It sold 301 veggie burgers and 259 nonveg burgers on Monday. On which day did it sell more?

(c) There are 9946 people in a town. If 4457 are men and 3962 are women, how many children are there?

(d) Ravi scored 9735 points in three games. In the first game he scored 3568, and in the second he scored 3983. What was his score in the third game?

Review Worksheet 2

1. Fill in.

   (a) The expanded form of 9783 is _____.

   (b) The greatest three-digit number formed with 5, 4 and 3 is _____.

   (c) The smallest three-digit number formed with 7, 9 and 0 is _____.

   (d) The number name of 8705 is _____.

   (e) Four thousand and forty in figures is _____.

   (f) In 7152, the place value of 7 is _____, that of 1 is _____ and that of 5 is _____.

   (g) In 157, the place value of 5 is _____, that of 1 is _____ and that of 7 is _____.

   (h) Write the numbers shown by the numerals: IV = _____ VII = _____ XX = _____.

   (i) Write in Roman numerals: 6 = _____ 8 = _____ 14 = _____.

   Do these sums.

2. (a)
```
  5 3 6 5
+ 2 1 7 8
```
   (b)
```
  3 4 2 8
+ 4 6 8 5
```
   (c)
```
  7 9 3 8
- 2 5 4 9
```
   (d)
```
  4 1 0 3
- 1 5 7 6
```

3. (a) 374 + 469 + 51   (b) 23 + 34 + 56 + 67   (c) 261 + 372 + 446   (d) 2137 + 4852 + 39

4. (a) 653 + 256 – 27   (b) 800 – 357– 206   (c) 3412 – 1281 + 5290

5. (a) In a day, a printer prints 6780 copies of the morning newspaper and 2135 copies of the evening newspaper. How many copies of the newspaper does he print in a day?

   (b) A farmer wants to plant 2740 trees. He has planted 1864. How many more trees does he have to plant?

   (c) Rekha recorded 3275 songs. Of these, 2138 were Hindi songs, 573 were Marathi and the rest were Bengali. How many Bengali songs did she record?

7. Multiplication

2 + 2 + 2 + 2 = 8 or 4 × 2 = 8

2 + 2 + 2 + 2 = 4 × 2 = 8

We say: 4 twos are 8
or 4 times 2 is 8.

3 + 3 + 3 + 3 + 3 = 15 or 5 × 3 = 15

3 + 3 + 3 + 3 + 3 = 5 × 3 = 15

We say: 5 threes are 15
or 5 times 3 is 15.

Multiplication is the repeated addition of a number. It is shown by the sign '×'.
The result of multiplication is called the product.
In 5 × 3 = 15, 15 is the product of 5 and 3. We say 5 and 3 are factors of 15.

Multiplication Facts

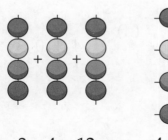

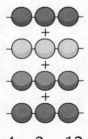

3 × 4 = 12   4 × 3 = 12

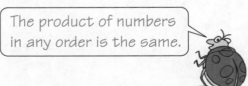

The product of numbers
in any order is the same.

3 × 4 = 12 = 4 × 3
5 × 3 = 15 = 3 × 5
6 × 7 = 42 = 7 × 6
7 × 8 = 56 = 8 × 7
8 × 5 = 40 = 5 × 8
9 × 6 = 54 = 6 × 9

0 + 0 + 0 + 0 + 0 = 0

5 × 0 = 0

So, 0 × 5 = 0

0 + 0 + 0 + 0 + 0 + 0 = 0

6 × 0 = 0

0 × 6 = 0

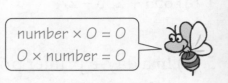

number × 0 = 0
0 × number = 0

number × 1 = same number
1 × number = same number

3 × 1 = 3   1 × 3 = 3
9 × 1 = 9   1 × 9 = 9
12 × 1 = 12   1 × 12 = 12

Multiplication Tables (1–10)

Add to build these tables.

1 × 1 = 1	2 × 1 = 2	3 × 1 = 3
1 × 2 = 2	2 × 2 = 4	3 × 2 = 6
1 × 3 = 3	2 × 3 = 6	3 × 3 = 9
1 × 4 = 4	2 × 4 = 8	3 × 4 = 12
1 × 5 = 5	2 × 5 = 10	3 × 5 = 15
1 × 6 = 6	2 × 6 = 12	3 × 6 = 18
1 × 7 = 7	2 × 7 = 14	3 × 7 = 21
1 × 8 = 8	2 × 8 = 16	3 × 8 = 24
1 × 9 = 9	2 × 9 = 18	3 × 9 = 27
1 × 10 = 10	2 × 10 = 20	3 × 10 = 30

4 (+4 each step: 4, 8, 12, ...)

4 × 1 = 4
4 × 2 = 8
4 × 3 =
4 × 4 =
4 × 5 =
4 × 6 =
4 × 7 =
4 × 8 =
4 × 9 =
4 × 10 =

5 (+5 each step: 5, 10, ...)

5 × 1 =
5 × 2 =
5 × 3 =
5 × 4 =
5 × 5 =
5 × 6 =
5 × 7 =
5 × 8 =
5 × 9 =
5 × 10 =

6 × 1 = 6	7 × 1 = 7	8 × 1 = 8
6 × 2 = 12	7 × 2 = 14	8 × 2 = 16
6 × 3 = 18	7 × 3 = 21	8 × 3 = 24
6 × 4 = 24	7 × 4 = 28	8 × 4 = 32
6 × 5 = 30	7 × 5 = 35	8 × 5 = 40
6 × 6 = 36	7 × 6 = 42	8 × 6 = 48
6 × 7 = 42	7 × 7 = 49	8 × 7 = 56
6 × 8 = 48	7 × 8 = 56	8 × 8 = 64
6 × 9 = 54	7 × 9 = 63	8 × 9 = 72
6 × 10 = 60	7 × 10 = 70	8 × 10 = 80

9 (+9 each step: 9, 18, 27, ...)

9 × 1 = 9
9 × 2 = 18
9 × 3 =
9 × 4 =
9 × 5 =
9 × 6 =
9 × 7 =
9 × 8 =
9 × 9 =
9 × 10 =

10 (+10 each step: 10, 20, ...)

10 × 1 =
10 × 2 =
10 × 3 =
10 × 4 =
10 × 5 =
10 × 6 =
10 × 7 =
10 × 8 =
10 × 9 =
10 × 10 =

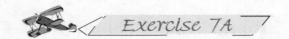

Fill in to show that multiplication is repeated addition.

2 + 2 + 2 + 2 = _____   6 + 6 + 6 + 6 + 6 = _____   8 + 8 + 8 = _____

__4__ × __2__ = _____   _____ × _____ = _____   _____ × _____ = _____

4 × 5 = _____   3 × 9 = _____   5 × 6 = _____

__5 +__ __+__ __+__ _____ = ___   _____ = ___   _____ = ___

Fill in.

4 × 5 = 5 × _____   8 × 6 = 6 × _____   9 × 8 = _____ × 9   7 × 10 = _____ × 7

8 × _____ = 8   25 × _____ = 25   _____ × 9 = 9   _____ × 12 = 12

6 × 0 = _____   _____ × 8 = 0   15 × 0 = _____   0 × 100 = _____

Multiply.

2 × 8 =   3 × 7 =   4 × 8 =   5 × 9 =

8 × 2 =   7 × 3 =   8 × 4 =   9 × 5 =

6 × 5 =   7 × 7 =   4 × 9 =   3 × 6 =

2 × 9 =   9 × 6 =   8 × 8 =   10 × 6 =

$$\begin{array}{r} 6 \\ \times\ 3 \\ \hline \end{array}$$ $$\begin{array}{r} 4 \\ \times\ 7 \\ \hline \end{array}$$ $$\begin{array}{r} 5 \\ \times\ 8 \\ \hline \end{array}$$ $$\begin{array}{r} 8 \\ \times\ 3 \\ \hline \end{array}$$ $$\begin{array}{r} 9 \\ \times\ 9 \\ \hline \end{array}$$

Fill in.

2 × _____ = 12   _____ × 3 = 24   6 × _____ = 30   _____ × 7 = 56

_____ × 5 = 35   4 × _____ = 16   _____ × 8 = 48   9 × _____ = 54

Multiplying 2-digit Numbers by 1-digit Numbers

Multiplying Tens by 1-digit Numbers

$40 \times 3 = 4$ tens $\times 3 = 3 \times 4$ tens
  $= 4$ tens $+ 4$ tens $+ 4$ tens
  $= 12$ tens $= 120$.

$\therefore \underline{40} \times \underline{3} = 120$.

Write 0 at the ones place. Multiply with the digit at the tens place.

Do these quickly.

| $20 \times 2 = 40$ | $40 \times 2 =$ | $50 \times 2 =$ | $80 \times 3 =$ |
| $30 \times 5 =$ | $40 \times 4 =$ | $60 \times 6 =$ | $90 \times 5 =$ |

Multiplying 2-digit Numbers by 1-digit Numbers

Multiply 23 by 2.

$23 \times 2 = 2$ tens $\times 2 + 3$ ones $\times 2$
  $= 4$ tens $+ 6$ ones $= 46$.

So multiply the ones first, then the tens.
O: $3 \times 2 = 6$
T: $2 \times 2 = 4$

```
  T O
  2 3
×   2
  4 6
```

Multiply 45 by 3.

$45 \times 3 = 4$ tens $\times 3 + 5$ ones $\times 3$
  $= 12$ tens $+ 15$ ones
  $= 12$ tens $+ 1$ ten $+ 5$ ones
  $= 13$ tens $+ 5$ ones
  $= \mathbf{1\ hundred} + 3$ tens $+ 5$ ones $= 135$.

Multiply right to left. At each place, after multiplying, add the carried number.

```
H T O
  1
  4 5
×   3
    5
```

O: $5 \times 3 = 15$
  $= 1$ ten $+ 5$ ones.
  Write 5 under O.
Carry 1 ten.

```
H T O
1 1
  4 5
×   3
1 3 5
```

T: $4 \times 3 = 12$
  $1 + 12 = 13$
  13 tens $= 10$ tens $+ 3$ tens
       $= 1$ hundred $+ 3$ tens.
Write 3 under T, carry 1 hundred.
H: $0 \times 3 + 1 = 0 + 1 = 1$

Do these sums.

1. (a)
```
   1 2
 ×   4
```
(b)
```
   1 3
 ×   3
```
(c)
```
   1 4
 ×   2
```
(d)
```
   1 1
 ×   6
```
(e)
```
   2 1
 ×   4
```

(f)
```
   2 0
 ×   3
```
(g)
```
   2 2
 ×   3
```
(h)
```
   3 4
 ×   2
```
(i)
```
   3 3
 ×   3
```
(j)
```
   4 2
 ×   2
```

2. (a)
```
   1 2
 ×   5
```
(b)
```
   1 4
 ×   6
```
(c)
```
   1 5
 ×   3
```
(d)
```
   1 3
 ×   7
```
(e)
```
   1 9
 ×   4
```

(f)
```
   2 7
 ×   3
```
(g)
```
   2 5
 ×   2
```
(h)
```
   2 6
 ×   3
```
(i)
```
   3 5
 ×   2
```
(j)
```
   4 6
 ×   2
```

3. (a)
```
   6 4
 ×   2
```
(b)
```
   5 8
 ×   2
```
(c)
```
   3 5
 ×   3
```
(d)
```
   4 6
 ×   4
```
(e)
```
   5 3
 ×   5
```

(f)
```
   6 2
 ×   6
```
(g)
```
   3 4
 ×   7
```
(h)
```
   7 5
 ×   2
```
(i)
```
   4 3
 ×   8
```
(j)
```
   8 6
 ×   9
```

4. Do these sums in your notebook.

(a) 14×4 (b) 15×6 (c) 16×7 (d) 18×5 (e) 23×4 (f) 34×6

(g) 45×6 (h) 57×3 (i) 49×8 (j) 64×9 (k) 77×7 (l) 92×8

1. A chessboard has 8 rows of 8 squares each. How many squares does it have in all?

2.  A toy needs 3 batteries. How many batteries are needed for 6 of these toys?

3. Teams from 9 schools took part in a quiz contest. Each team had 4 members. How many children took part in the contest?

4. A CD box holds 12 CDs. How many CDs will 8 such boxes have?

5. Do these sums in your notebook.

   (a) Adil has a piece of squared paper. The piece has 11 rows and 9 columns of squares. How many squares does it have in all?

   (b) A paint box has 16 tubes of paints. How many tubes will 5 such boxes have?

   (c) A day has 24 hours. How many hours does a week have?

   (d) Piya's school was closed for 45 days for summer holidays. Every day she did 6 sums. How many sums did she do during the holidays?

   (e) The calendar for a month has 4 rows. Each row has 7 days. Which month's calendar is it?

Multiplying 3-digit Numbers by 1-digit Numbers

Th	H	T	O
	4	9³	6
×			5
			0

O: $6 \times 5 = 30$
Write 0, carry 3 tens.

Th	H	T	O
	4	9³	6
×			5
		8	0

T: $9 \times 5 = 45$
$3 + 45 = 48$
Write 8.
Carry 4 hundreds.

Th	H	T	O
	2⁴	9³	6
×			5
2	4	8	0

H: $4 \times 5 = 20$
$4 + 20 = 24$
Write 4.
Carry 2 thousands.
Th: $0 \times 5 + 2 = 2$

Exercise 7D

Multiply.

1. (a)
```
  1 1 2
×     2
```
(b)
```
  2 1 3
×     2
```
(c)
```
  4 0 4
×     2
```
(d)
```
  3 2 1
×     3
```
(e)
```
  1 0 0
×     9
```

2. (a)
```
  2 1 8
×     2
```
(b)
```
  3 4 5
×     2
```
(c)
```
  1 3 4
×     3
```
(d)
```
  2 6 5
×     3
```
(e)
```
  3 0 7
×     4
```

(f)
```
  2 1 8
×     4
```
(g)
```
  1 9 5
×     5
```
(h)
```
  1 1 6
×     8
```
(i)
```
  3 0 9
×     3
```
(j)
```
  1 0 8
×     7
```

3. (a)
```
  1 1 2
×     9
```
(b)
```
  1 7 8
×     6
```
(c)
```
  2 0 4
×     5
```
(d)
```
  3 4 5
×     3
```
(e)
```
  4 6 8
×     4
```

(f)
```
  5 9 8
×     5
```
(g)
```
  6 4 3
×     9
```
(h)
```
  2 5 8
×     7
```
(i)
```
  4 1 5
×     8
```
(j)
```
  6 0 6
×     6
```

4. (a) 214×3 (b) 423×4 (c) 572×5 (d) 182×6 (e) 641×4 (f) 789×2

Multiplication Tables (11—20)

Add 11s to build the table of 11.

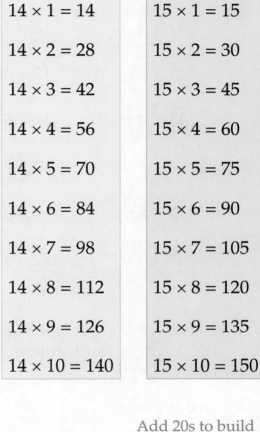

11 × 1 = 11	12 × 1 = 12	13 × 1 = 13	14 × 1 = 14	15 × 1 = 15
11 × 2 = 22	12 × 2 = 24	13 × 2 = 26	14 × 2 = 28	15 × 2 = 30
11 × 3 =	12 × 3 = 36	13 × 3 = 39	14 × 3 = 42	15 × 3 = 45
11 × 4 =	12 × 4 = 48	13 × 4 = 52	14 × 4 = 56	15 × 4 = 60
11 × 5 =	12 × 5 = 60	13 × 5 = 65	14 × 5 = 70	15 × 5 = 75
11 × 6 =	12 × 6 = 72	13 × 6 = 78	14 × 6 = 84	15 × 6 = 90
11 × 7 =	12 × 7 = 84	13 × 7 = 91	14 × 7 = 98	15 × 7 = 105
11 × 8 =	12 × 8 = 96	13 × 8 = 104	14 × 8 = 112	15 × 8 = 120
11 × 9 =	12 × 9 = 108	13 × 9 = 117	14 × 9 = 126	15 × 9 = 135
11 × 10 =	12 × 10 = 120	13 × 10 = 130	14 × 10 = 140	15 × 10 = 150

Add 20s to build the table of 20.

16 × 1 = 16	17 × 1 = 17	18 × 1 = 18	19 × 1 = 19	20 × 1 = 20
16 × 2 = 32	17 × 2 = 34	18 × 2 = 36	19 × 2 = 38	20 × 2 = 40
16 × 3 = 48	17 × 3 = 51	18 × 3 = 54	19 × 3 = 57	20 × 3 =
16 × 4 = 64	17 × 4 = 68	18 × 4 = 72	19 × 4 = 76	20 × 4 =
16 × 5 = 80	17 × 5 = 85	18 × 5 = 90	19 × 5 = 95	20 × 5 = 100
16 × 6 = 96	17 × 6 = 102	18 × 6 = 108	19 × 6 = 114	20 × 6 =
16 × 7 = 112	17 × 7 = 119	18 × 7 = 126	19 × 7 = 133	20 × 7 =
16 × 8 = 128	17 × 8 = 136	18 × 8 = 144	19 × 8 = 152	20 × 8 =
16 × 9 = 144	17 × 9 = 153	18 × 9 = 162	19 × 9 = 171	20 × 9 =
16 × 10 = 160	17 × 10 = 170	18 × 10 = 180	19 × 10 = 190	20 × 10 =

Do these after learning tables up to 15.

	12 × 2 =	13 × 2 =	14 × 2 =	15 × 2 =

12 × 3 =	13 × 3 =	14 × 3 =	15 × 3 =

11 × 2 =	12 × 4 =	13 × 4 =	14 × 4 =	15 × 4 =
11 × 3 =	12 × 5 =	13 × 5 =	14 × 5 =	15 × 5 =
11 × 4 =	12 × 6 =	13 × 6 =	14 × 6 =	15 × 6 =
11 × 5 =	12 × 7 =	13 × 7 =	14 × 7 =	15 × 7 =
11 × 8 =	12 × 8 =	13 × 8 =	14 × 8 =	15 × 8 =
11 × 9 =	12 × 9 =	13 × 9 =	14 × 9 =	15 × 9 =

Multiplication by Tens, Hundreds and Thousands

$49 \times 10 = 49$ tens
$\qquad = 490$

$60 \times 10 = 60$ tens
$\qquad = 600$

$35 \times 100 = 35$ hundreds
$\qquad = 3500$

$70 \times 100 = 70$ hundreds
$\qquad = 7000$

$6 \times 1000 = 6$ thousands
$\qquad = 6000$

❶ Count the zeros on the right of the numbers.

❷ Multiply the digits on the left of the zeros.

❸ Write their product followed by the number of zeros counted in ❶ .

$14 \times 40 = 14 \times 4 \times 10$
$\qquad = 56 \times 10$
$\qquad = 56$ tens
$\qquad = 560$

$12 \times 300 = 12 \times 3 \times 100$
$\qquad = 36 \times 100$
$\qquad = 36$ hundreds
$\qquad = 3600$

$4 \times 2000 = 4 \times 2 \times 1000$
$\qquad = 8 \times 1000$
$\qquad = 8$ thousands
$\qquad = 8000$

$$\begin{array}{r} \overset{1}{2\ 4} \\ \times\ 3\ 0 \\ \hline 720 \end{array}$$

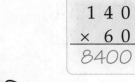

❶ Zeros on the right: 1.
❷ Find 24 × 3.
❸ Put 1 zero on the right of the product.

$$\begin{array}{r} 1\ 4\ 0 \\ \times\ \ 6\ 0 \\ \hline 8400 \end{array}$$

❶ Zeros on the right: 2.
❷ Find 14 × 6.
❸ Put 2 zeros on the right of the product.

$$\begin{array}{r} 2\ 0\overset{1}{5} \\ \times\ \ \ 3\ 0 \\ \hline 6150 \end{array}$$

Put 1 zero on the right of the product of 205 and 3.

$$\begin{array}{r} 1\ 3 \\ \times 2\ 0\ 0 \\ \hline 2600 \end{array}$$

Put 2 zeros on the right of the product of 13 and 2.

Exercise 7E

Multiply.

1. (a) 84 × 10 =   (b) 62 × 10 =   (c) 96 × 10 =   (d) 123 × 10 =

(e) 342 × 10 =   (f) 608 × 10 =   (g) 3 × 30 =   (h) 4 × 50 =

(i) 7 × 40 =   (j) 12 × 20 =   (k) 15 × 30 =   (l) 11 × 90 =

2. (a) 7 × 100 =   (b) 25 × 100 =   (c) 10 × 100 =   (d) 87 × 100 =

(e) 40 × 100 =   (f) 65 × 100 =   (g) 5 × 300 =   (h) 9 × 600 =

(i) 8 × 500 =   (j) 7 × 900 =   (k) 14 × 200 =   (l) 12 × 400 =

(m) 13 × 300 =   (n) 14 × 500 =   (o) 15 × 200 =   (p) 15 × 600 =

3. (a) 2 × 1000 =   (b) 4 × 1000 =   (c) 6 × 1000 =   (d) 9 × 1000 =

(e) 3 × 2000 =   (f) 2 × 3000 =   (g) 4 × 2000 =   (h) 2 × 2000 =

4. (a)
$$\begin{array}{r} 1\ 4 \\ \times\ 6\ 0 \\ \hline \end{array}$$

(b)
$$\begin{array}{r} 1\ 5 \\ \times\ 8\ 0 \\ \hline \end{array}$$

(c)
$$\begin{array}{r} 1\ 6 \\ \times\ 7\ 0 \\ \hline \end{array}$$

(d)
$$\begin{array}{r} 1\ 8 \\ \times\ 6\ 0 \\ \hline \end{array}$$

(e)
$$\begin{array}{r} 1\ 9 \\ \times\ 9\ 0 \\ \hline \end{array}$$

(f)
$$\begin{array}{r} 1\ 3 \\ \times\ 7\ 0 \\ \hline \end{array}$$

(g)
$$\begin{array}{r} 2\ 1 \\ \times\ 4\ 0 \\ \hline \end{array}$$

(h)
$$\begin{array}{r} 2\ 3 \\ \times\ 5\ 0 \\ \hline \end{array}$$

(i)
$$\begin{array}{r} 3\ 4 \\ \times\ 7\ 0 \\ \hline \end{array}$$

(j)
$$\begin{array}{r} 8\ 0 \\ \times\ 8\ 0 \\ \hline \end{array}$$

(k)
$$\begin{array}{r} 6\ 8 \\ \times\ 3\ 0 \\ \hline \end{array}$$

(l)
$$\begin{array}{r} 7\ 4 \\ \times\ 2\ 0 \\ \hline \end{array}$$

5. (a)
$$\begin{array}{r} 1\ 2\ 3 \\ \times\ \ \ 4\ 0 \\ \hline \end{array}$$

(b)
$$\begin{array}{r} 1\ 5\ 0 \\ \times\ \ \ 2\ 0 \\ \hline \end{array}$$

(c)
$$\begin{array}{r} 1\ 5\ 2 \\ \times\ \ \ 3\ 0 \\ \hline \end{array}$$

(d)
$$\begin{array}{r} 3\ 5\ 4 \\ \times\ \ \ 2\ 0 \\ \hline \end{array}$$

(e)
$$\begin{array}{r} 2\ 6\ 7 \\ \times\ \ \ 3\ 0 \\ \hline \end{array}$$

(f)
$$\begin{array}{r} 1\ 0\ 7 \\ \times\ \ \ 8\ 0 \\ \hline \end{array}$$

(g)
$$\begin{array}{r} 1\ 4\ 0 \\ \times\ \ \ 6\ 0 \\ \hline \end{array}$$

(h)
$$\begin{array}{r} 4\ 0\ 0 \\ \times\ \ \ 2\ 0 \\ \hline \end{array}$$

(i)
$$\begin{array}{r} 3\ 1\ 9 \\ \times\ \ \ 3\ 0 \\ \hline \end{array}$$

(j)
$$\begin{array}{r} 1\ 2\ 4 \\ \times\ \ \ 7\ 0 \\ \hline \end{array}$$

6. (a)
$$\begin{array}{r} 1\ 5 \\ \times\ 4\ 0\ 0 \\ \hline \end{array}$$

(b)
$$\begin{array}{r} 1\ 8 \\ \times\ 3\ 0\ 0 \\ \hline \end{array}$$

(c)
$$\begin{array}{r} 1\ 9 \\ \times\ 4\ 0\ 0 \\ \hline \end{array}$$

(d)
$$\begin{array}{r} 2\ 0 \\ \times\ 4\ 0\ 0 \\ \hline \end{array}$$

(e)
$$\begin{array}{r} 2\ 5 \\ \times\ 3\ 0\ 0 \\ \hline \end{array}$$

(f)
$$\begin{array}{r} 2\ 7 \\ \times\ 2\ 0\ 0 \\ \hline \end{array}$$

(g)
$$\begin{array}{r} 3\ 2 \\ \times\ 3\ 0\ 0 \\ \hline \end{array}$$

(h)
$$\begin{array}{r} 3\ 6 \\ \times\ 2\ 0\ 0 \\ \hline \end{array}$$

(i)
$$\begin{array}{r} 4\ 4 \\ \times\ 2\ 0\ 0 \\ \hline \end{array}$$

(j)
$$\begin{array}{r} 2\ 8 \\ \times\ 3\ 0\ 0 \\ \hline \end{array}$$

Do these sums in your notebook.

7. (a) 46×80 (b) 38×90 (c) 26×70 (d) 93×40 (e) 66×50 (f) 57×60

8. (a) 152×30 (b) 196×50 (c) 115×60 (d) 230×30 (e) 436×20 (f) 104×90

2-digit Number x 2-digit Number

Multiply 28 by 23.

$23 = 2$ tens $+ 3$ ones $= 20 + 3$

$28 \times 23 = 28 \times 2$ tens $+ 3$ ones

$\quad\quad\quad = 28 \times 20 + 3$

$\quad\quad\quad = 28 \times 20 + 28 \times 3$

$\quad\quad\quad = 560 + 84$

$\quad\quad\quad = 644.$

```
    H T O
      2 8
   ×  2 3
❶     8 4
❷   5 6 0
❸   6 4 4
```

❶ 28 x ones: 28 x 3
❷ 28 x tens: 28 x 20 *
❸ Add the two products.

*At ❷, you can think
28 x 2 tens = 56 tens
= 5 hundreds and 6 tens,
and write as shown ⟶ .

```
    H T O
      2 8
   ×  2 3
❶     8 4
❷   5 6
❸   6 4 4
```

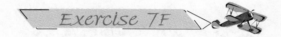

Exercise 7F

Multiply.

1. (a)
```
    1 2
 ×  1 1
 _____
```

(b)
```
    1 4
 ×  1 3
 _____
```

(c)
```
    1 6
 ×  1 6
 _____
```

(d)
```
    2 3
 ×  1 5
 _____
```

(e)
```
    3 4
 ×  2 5
 _____
```

(f)
```
    4 2
 ×  1 9
 _____
```

(g)
```
    5 6
 ×  3 2
 _____
```

(h)
```
    6 4
 ×  4 3
 _____
```

(i)
```
    7 6
 ×  4 5
 _____
```

(j)
```
    8 4
 ×  6 8
 _____
```

Do these sums in your notebook.

2. (a) 11×22 (b) 23×31 (c) 33×13 (d) 43×12 (e) 32×23 (f) 21×34

3. (a) 25×14 (b) 36×17 (c) 57×18 (d) 67×24 (e) 75×36 (f) 25×25

4. (a) 28×36 (b) 49×32 (c) 66×49 (d) 82×56 (e) 97×21 (f) 78×65

3-digit Number x 2-digit Number

Multiply 324 by 28.

Th	H	T	O
	3	2	4
	×	2	8

❶ 2 5 9 2
❷ 6 4 8 0
❸ 9 0 7 2

❶ 324 x ones: 324 x 8
❷ 324 x tens: 324 x 20 *
❸ Add the two products.

*❷: 324 x 2 tens = 648 tens,
= 6 thousands, 4 hundreds
and 8 tens, as shown ⟶ .

Th	H	T	O
	3	2	4
	×	2	8

❶ 2 5 9 2
❷ 6 4 8
❸ 9 0 7 2

Exercise 7G

Multiply.

1. (a)
```
  1 2 6
×   1 2
_____
```

(b)
```
  1 4 7
×   1 3
_____
```

(c)
```
  2 4 5
×   1 4
_____
```

(d)
```
  2 0 8
×   1 5
_____
```

(e)
```
  2 9 3
×   1 6
_____
```

(f)
```
  3 0 5
×   1 7
_____
```

(g)
```
  4 1 8
×   1 8
_____
```

(h)
```
  5 1 3
×   1 9
_____
```

(i)
```
  7 6 3
×   1 3
_____
```

(j)
```
  2 9 0
×   2 5
_____
```

(k)
```
  3 1 6
×   2 8
_____
```

(l)
```
  3 4 2
×   3 1
_____
```

(m)
```
  1 8 7
×   3 4
_____
```

(n)
```
  2 1 6
×   3 7
_____
```

(o)
```
  1 9 8
×   4 8
_____
```

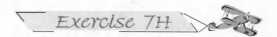

1. 47 children sent 20 New Year cards each. How many cards did they send in all?

2.  If a packet has 52 balloons, how many balloons will 24 such packets have?

3. A box has a dozen (12) eggs. How many eggs do 35 such boxes have?

4. A man buys 36 bananas for his monkeys every day. How many bananas does he buy in a month (30 days)?

5. Do these sums in your notebook.

   (a) The heart beats 72 times a minute. How many times does it beat in 60 minutes?

   (b) If a day has 24 hours, how many hours does a month have?

   (c) An apartment block has 186 flats. How many flats will 8 such blocks have?

   (d) Birju delivers 150 packets of milk every day. How many packets does he deliver in 15 days?

   (e) Mr Menon reads 12 pages of the morning newspaper every day. How many pages of the newspaper does he read in a year (365 days)?

MathGym

The teacher will call out the clues. Children will tick the answers.
The one who gets it all correct first wins.

50	700	999
111	64	100
4	600	81
60	9999	3

Clues

- Hundred ones
- Nine times nine
- The difference between 85 and 21
- 47 plus 13
- The number before 10,000
- 300 plus what is 1000?
- This number added 3 times gives 12
- This multiplied by 2 gives 100

Add the rows and columns. Then add the numbers you get. Their sums will be the same. Magic? Or the sum of 4 numbers? Make your own magic boxes and see.

3	2	5
5	4	9
8	6	14

4	8	
12	6	

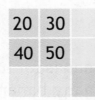

20	30	
40	50	

Fill in.

8	×	2	=	

8	×		=	16

	×	2	=	16

9	×	4	=	

9	×		=	36

4	×		=	36

12	×	2	=	

	×	12	=	24

	×	3	=	24

7	×		=	56

7	×		=	560

12	×		=	240

	×	9	=	81

9	×		=	810

12	×		=	2400

200	×		=	600

119	×		=	0

181	×		=	181

Do and Learn

Aim To introduce division

Things needed Beads, paper clips, sheets of paper

Do and Learn

1. Take 6 paper clips or beads. You have to divide them equally among 3 sheets of paper.

6 clips

2. Put a clip on each sheet. You will be left with 3 clips to divide.

$6 - 3 = 3$

3. Divide the remaining clips. You will be left with 0 clips. The 6 clips have been divided equally among 3 sheets. Each sheet got 2.

$3 - 3 = 0$

We say: 6 divided by 3 is 2. We write: $6 \div 3 = 2$.

$\div$ is the sign of division. 6 is the dividend, 3 is the divisor and 2 is the quotient.

Note that   Dividend = Divisor x Quotient. $(6 = 3 \times 2)$

Division is repeated subtraction.

$6 \div 3 = 2$ means: 3 can be subtracted 2 times from 6 .

4. Now take 9 beads (or clips) and divide them between 4 sheets.

9 beads

5. Put a bead on each sheet. You are left with 5 beads to divide.

$9 - 4 = 5$

6. Again put a bead on each sheet. You will be left with 1 bead. You cannot divide it among the 4 sheets. It is the remainder after the division.

$5 - 4 = 1$

We say: 9 divided by 4 is 2, with remainder 1.

Here,   Dividend = Divisor x Quotient + Remainder. $(9 = 4 \times 2 + 1)$

73

8. Division

Divide by repeated subtraction.

15 ÷ 5
15 − 5 = 10
10 − 5 = 5
5 − 5 = 0
∴ 15 ÷ 5 = 3
(5 can be subtracted 3 times from 15.)

9 ÷ 3

12 ÷ 3

36 ÷ 9

40 ÷ 10

35 ÷ 7

Divide into equal groups by drawing by turn in the boxes.

15 ÷ 3

15 ÷ 3 = 5

If 15 is divided into 3 equal groups, each group gets 5.

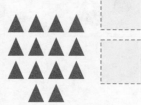

16 ÷ 4

14 ÷ 2

18 ÷ 6

74

Division and Multiplication are Related

Multiplication Fact

2 threes are 6.
$2 \times 3 = 6$

3 fours are 12.
$3 \times 4 = 12$

Division Fact

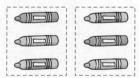

6 crayons divided into 2 equal groups gives 3 crayons in each.
$6 \div 2 = 3$

12 hats divided into 3 equal groups gives 4 hats in each.
$12 \div 3 = 4$

Division Fact

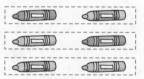

6 crayons divided into 3 equal groups gives 2 crayons in each.
$6 \div 3 = 2$

12 hats divided into 4 equal groups gives 3 hats in each.
$12 \div 4 = 3$

Multiplication facts give division facts.
So, for division, we use multiplication tables.

$$7 \times 0 = 0 \qquad\qquad 8 \times 1 = 8$$
$$\therefore \quad 0 \div 7 = 0 \qquad\qquad 8 \div 8 = 1$$
$$8 \div 1 = 8$$

$0 \div$ counting number $= 0$
number $\div$ same number $= 1$
number $\div 1 =$ same number

Write division facts.

$15 \times 3 = 45$	$8 \times 4 = 32$	$7 \times 8 = 56$	$9 \times 5 = 45$
$45 \div 15 = 3$ $45 \div 3 = 15$			

$11 \times 9 = 99$	$12 \times 6 = 72$	$13 \times 7 = 91$	$14 \times 1 = 14$

Fill in.

$39 \div 13 =$ ____

Think
$13 \times ? = 39$

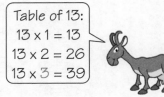

Table of 13:
$13 \times 1 = 13$
$13 \times 2 = 26$
$13 \times 3 = 39$

$39 \div 13 = \underline{3}$

Exercise 8A

Fill in.

$8 \div 2 =$	$14 \div 2 =$	$18 \div 2 =$	$9 \div 3 =$
$15 \div 3 =$	$21 \div 3 =$	$16 \div 4 =$	$24 \div 4 =$
$15 \div 5 =$	$25 \div 5 =$	$45 \div 5 =$	$24 \div 6 =$
$36 \div 6 =$	$42 \div 6 =$	$42 \div 7 =$	$35 \div 7 =$
$32 \div 8 =$	$48 \div 8 =$	$64 \div 8 =$	$72 \div 8 =$
$36 \div 9 =$	$54 \div 9 =$	$63 \div 9 =$	$72 \div 9 =$
$70 \div 7 =$	$50 \div 10 =$	$22 \div 11 =$	$24 \div 12 =$
$36 \div 12 =$	$60 \div 12 =$	$26 \div 13 =$	$52 \div 13 =$
$56 \div 14 =$	$28 \div 14 =$	$60 \div 15 =$	$45 \div 15 =$

Fill in.

$5 \div 1 =$ ____ $0 \div 9 =$ ____ $7 \div 7 =$ ____ $14 \div 14 =$ ___ $25 \div 25 =$ ___

$0 \div 20 =$ ____ $99 \div 1 =$ ____ $56 \div 56 =$ ____ $18 \div 1 =$ ____ $0 \div 32 =$ ____

Long Division

Division can be shown in different ways.

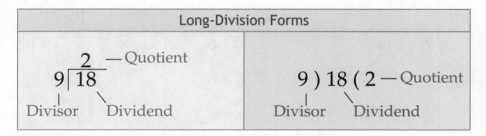

Dividend   Quotient

$18 \div 9 = 2$

Divisor

Long-Division Forms	
2 — Quotient 9⟌18 Divisor Dividend	9) 18 (2 — Quotient Divisor Dividend

We use long division for sums that need more than one step.

2-digit Number ÷ 1-digit Number

Divide 28 by 2 and check the answer.

$28 \div 2 =$ 2 tens + 8 ones $\div 2 =$ 2 tens $\div 2$ + 8 ones $\div 2$.

We shall divide in 2 steps, as shown below.

❶
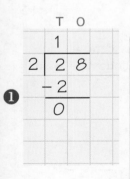

```
   T O
   1
 2|2 8
  -2
   0
```

2 x ? = 2   2 x 1 = 2
So, 2 tens ÷ 2 = 1 ten, or
2 tens can be subtracted
1 times from 2 tens.
T: Write 1 as the quotient
   of this step.
   Write 2 under the
   dividend and subtract.

❷
```
   T O
   1 4
 2|2 8
  -2↓
   0 8
    -8
     0
```

Now divide 8 ones by 2.
Bring down 8 ones.
2 x ? = 8   2 x 4 = 8
So, 8 ones ÷ 2 = 4 ones.
O: Write 4 as the quotient.
   Write 8 under the new
   dividend and subtract.

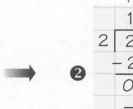

So, 28 ÷ 2 = 14. The answer is correct if
divisor x quotient = dividend.
As 2 x 14 = 28, the answer is correct.

Divide 63 by 3.

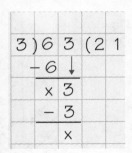

```
 3)6 3 (2 1
  -6↓
   x 3
  -3
   x
```

Let us write this division in a different way.
❶ 3 x ? = 6   3 x 2 = 6   So, 6 tens ÷ 3 = 2 tens.
   T: Write 2 as the quotient. Write 6 under the dividend. Subtract.
     The difference is zero. You can write x instead of 0.
❷ Bring down 3 ones.   3 x ? = 3   3 x 1 = 3
   O: Write 1 as the quotient of this division step.
     Write 3 under the new dividend and subtract.

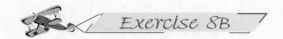
1. Divide and check the answer.

(a)

2 | 2 4

Dividend =
Quotient × Divisor =

(b)

3 | 6 9

Dividend =
Quotient × Divisor =

(c)

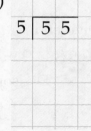
4 | 8 4

Dividend =
Quotient × Divisor =

(d)

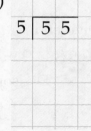
5 | 5 5

Dividend =
Quotient × Divisor =

(e)

2 | 4 6

Dividend =
Quotient × Divisor =

(f)

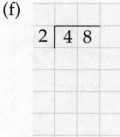
2 | 4 8

Dividend =
Quotient × Divisor =

(g)

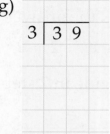
3 | 3 9

Dividend =
Quotient × Divisor =

(h)

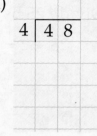
4 | 4 8

Dividend =
Quotient × Divisor =

2. Divide and check the answer.

(a) $26 \div 2$

Dividend =
Quotient × Divisor =

(b) $36 \div 3$

Dividend =
Quotient × Divisor =

(c) $86 \div 2$

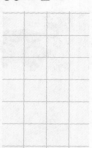

Dividend =
Quotient × Divisor =

(d) $77 \div 7$

Dividend =
Quotient × Divisor =

3. Divide and check the answer.

(a) $82 \div 2$ (b) $96 \div 3$ (c) $88 \div 8$ (d) $93 \div 3$

<u>3-digit Number ÷ 1-digit Number</u>

Divide 369 by 3.

$369 \div 3 = 3$ hundreds $\div 3 + 6$ tens $\div 3 + 9$ ones $\div 3$. We shall divide in 3 steps.

H T O
```
        1 2 3
    3 | 3 6 9
      - 3 ↓
        0 6
        - 6 ↓
          0 9
          - 9
            0
```

❶ 3 hundreds ÷ 3 = 1 hundred.
   H: Write 1 as the quotient. Write 3 under the dividend and subtract.

❷ Bring down 6 tens.   6 tens ÷ 3 = 2 tens.
   T: Write 2 as the quotient of this division step.
      Write 6 under the new dividend and subtract.

❸ Bring down 9 ones.   9 ones ÷ 3 = 3 ones.
   O: Write 3 as the quotient of this division step.
      Write 9 under the new dividend and subtract.

∴ 369 ÷ 3 = 123.

Divide 402 by 2.

H T O
```
        2 0 1
    2 | 4 0 2
      - 4 ↓
        0 0
        - 0 ↓
          0 2
          - 2
            0
```

❶ H: 4 ÷ 2 = 2
❷ Bring down 0 tens.
   T: 0 ÷ 2 = 0
❸ Bring down 2 ones.
   O: 2 ÷ 2 = 1

∴ 402 ÷ 2 = 201.

❶ H: 4 ÷ 4 = 1
❷ Bring down 8 tens.
   T: 8 ÷ 4 = 2
❸ Bring down 0 ones.
   O: 0 ÷ 4 = 0

Divide 480 by 4.

H T O
```
        1 2 0
    4 | 4 8 0
      - 4 ↓
        0 8 ↓
        - 8 ↓
          0 0
          - 0
            0
```

∴ 480 ÷ 4 = 120.

Divide 900 by 3.

H T O
```
        3 0 0
    3 | 9 0 0
      - 9 ↓
        0 0
        - 0 ↓
          0 0
          - 0
            0
```

❶ H: 9 ÷ 3 = 3
❷ Bring down 0 tens.
   T: 0 ÷ 3 = 0
❸ Bring down 0 ones.
   O: 0 ÷ 3 = 0

∴ 900 ÷ 3 = 300.

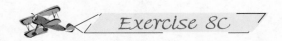

Divide.

1. (a)

   2 | 4 8 4

   (b)

   3 | 6 9 3

   (c)

   4 | 4 4 8

   (d)

   2 | 8 0 4

   (e)

   3 | 3 0 6

   (f)

   3 | 6 9 0

   (g)

   4 | 4 4 0

   (h)

   4 | 8 0 0

2. (a) $555 \div 5$ (b) $246 \div 2$ (c) $848 \div 4$ (d) $399 \div 3$

3. (a) $408 \div 4$ (b) $208 \div 2$ (c) $604 \div 2$ (d) $505 \div 5$

4. (a) $240 \div 2$ (b) $480 \div 2$ (c) $690 \div 3$ (d) $360 \div 3$

5. (a) $400 \div 2$ (b) $600 \div 2$ (c) $800 \div 2$ (d) $600 \div 3$

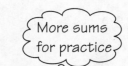
More sums for practice

6. (a) $242 \div 2$ (b) $888 \div 8$ (c) $936 \div 3$ (d) $648 \div 2$

7. (a) $609 \div 3$ (b) $903 \div 3$ (c) $909 \div 9$ (d) $404 \div 2$

8. (a) $840 \div 4$ (b) $660 \div 6$ (c) $420 \div 2$ (d) $960 \div 3$

9. (a) $300 \div 3$ (b) $500 \div 5$ (c) $700 \div 7$ (d) $900 \div 9$

4-digit Number ÷ 1-digit Number

Divide 4682 by 2.

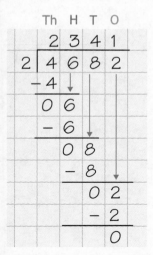

∴ 4682 ÷ 2 = 2341.

Divide 2004 by 2.

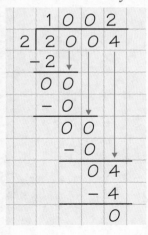

∴ 2004 ÷ 2 = 1002.

Divide 9600 by 3.

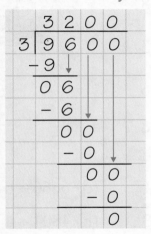

∴ 9600 ÷ 3 = 3200.

To divide 4-digit numbers, follow these steps:

❶ Divide the thousands.

❷ Divide the hundreds.

❸ Divide the tens.

❹ Divide the ones.

Divide 3903 by 3.

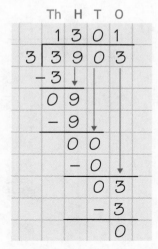

∴ 3903 ÷ 3 = 1301.

Divide 4840 by 4.

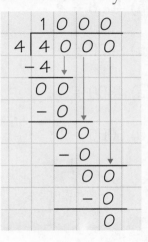

∴ 4840 ÷ 4 = 1210.

Divide 4000 by 4.

∴ 4000 ÷ 4 = 1000.

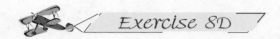

Divide.

1. (a)

$$2\overline{\smash{)}2468}$$

(b)

$$4\overline{\smash{)}4884}$$

(c)

$$3\overline{\smash{)}3693}$$

(d)

$$4\overline{\smash{)}8084}$$

(e)

$$2\overline{\smash{)}4002}$$

(f)

$$3\overline{\smash{)}6090}$$

(g)

$$2\overline{\smash{)}8600}$$

(h)

$$3\overline{\smash{)}6000}$$

2. (a) 2664 ÷ 2   (b) 4624 ÷ 2   (c) 6842 ÷ 2   (d) 8482 ÷ 2

3. (a) 2408 ÷ 2   (b) 4062 ÷ 2   (c) 6096 ÷ 3   (d) 8408 ÷ 4

4. (a) 4008 ÷ 2   (b) 6009 ÷ 3   (c) 8004 ÷ 4   (d) 8008 ÷ 8

5. (a) 8420 ÷ 2   (b) 3930 ÷ 3   (c) 4880 ÷ 4   (d) 5550 ÷ 5

6. (a) 4800 ÷ 2   (b) 6300 ÷ 3   (c) 8400 ÷ 4   (d) 6600 ÷ 6

7. (a) 6000 ÷ 2   (b) 9000 ÷ 3   (c) 8000 ÷ 4   (d) 9000 ÷ 9

More sums for practice

8. (a) 6393 ÷ 3   (b) 3969 ÷ 3   (c) 8448 ÷ 4   (d) 6666 ÷ 6

(e) 8402 ÷ 2   (f) 9006 ÷ 3   (g) 9300 ÷ 3   (h) 4804 ÷ 4

Division with Remainder

Divide 7 marbles between 2 boxes.
Each box will get 3 marbles.
You will be left with 1 marble, which cannot be divided between 2 boxes.

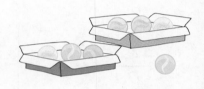

Dividend = 7   Divisor = 2   Quotient = 3   Remainder = 1

$$7 = 2 \times 3 + 1$$

Dividend = Divisor × Quotient + Remainder

Divide 9 by 4.

$4 \times ? = 9$ From multiplication tables, $4 \times 2 = 8$ and $4 \times 3 = 12$.

But $8 < 9$ and $12 > 9$.

So, 4 can only be subtracted 2 times from 9, leaving 1 as remainder.

So, dividend = 9, divisor = 4, quotient (Q) = 2 and remainder (R) = 1.

Divide 25 by 2 and check the answer.

```
    T O
    1 2
2 | 2 5
   -2
    0 5
   - 4
      1
```

T: $2 \div 2 = 1$. Q = 1

O: $5 \div 2 = ?$
    $2 \times 3 = 6$. $6 > 5$
    $2 \times 2 = 4$. $4 < 5$
    So, Q = 2,
        R = $5 - 4 = 1$.

$25 \div 2 = 12$ and remainder 1.

Divisor × quotient + remainder
   = $2 \times 12 + 1 = 24 + 1 = 25$ = dividend.
So the answer is correct.

Divide 368 by 3.

```
    H T O
    1 2 2
3 | 3 6 8
   -3
    0 6
   - 6
      0 8
     - 6
        2
```

H: $3 \div 3 = 1$.
T: $6 \div 3 = 2$.
O: $8 \div 3 = ?$
    $3 \times 3 = 9$. $9 > 8$
    $3 \times 2 = 6$. $6 < 8$
    So, Q = 2,
        R = $8 - 6 = 2$.

$368 \div 3 = 122$ and remainder 2.

Divide 481 by 2.

```
        H  T  O
        2  4  0
  2 |   4  8  1
      -  4
        0  8
      -  8
        0  1
      -  0
           1
```

H: $4 \div 2 = 2$
T: $8 \div 2 = 4$
O: $1 \div 2 = ?$
$\quad 2 \times 1 = 2. \quad 2 > 1$
$\quad 2 \times 0 = 0. \quad 0 < 1$
So, $Q = 0$,
$\quad\quad R = 1 - 0 = 1.$

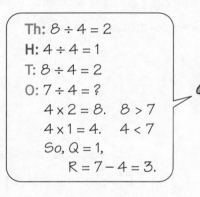

$481 \div 2 = 240$ and remainder 1.

Divide 609 by 6.

```
        H  T  O
        1  0  1
  6 |   6  0  9
      -  6
        0  0
      -  0
        0  9
      -  6
           3
```

$609 \div 6 = 101$ and remainder 3.

Divide 8487 by 4.

```
     2  1  2  1
  4 | 8  4  8  7
    - 8
      0  4
    -    4
      0  8
    -    8
      0  7
    -    4
         3
```

Th: $8 \div 4 = 2$
H: $4 \div 4 = 1$
T: $8 \div 4 = 2$
O: $7 \div 4 = ?$
$\quad 4 \times 2 = 8. \quad 8 > 7$
$\quad 4 \times 1 = 4. \quad 4 < 7$
So, $Q = 1$,
$\quad\quad R = 7 - 4 = 3.$

$8487 \div 4 = 2121$ and remainder 3.

Divide 5504 by 5.

```
     1  1  0  0
  5 | 5  5  0  4
    - 5
      0  5
    -    5
      0  0
    -    0
      0  4
    -    0
         4
```

$5504 \div 5 = 1100$ and remainder 4.

Divide 7008 by 7.

```
     1  0  0  1
  7 | 7  0  0  8
    - 7
      0  0
    -    0
      0  0
    -    0
      0  8
    -    7
         1
```

$7008 \div 7 = 1001$ and
remainder 1.

Divide 8041 by 2.

```
     4  0  2  0
  2 | 8  0  4  1
    - 8
      0  0
    -    0
      0  4
    -    4
      0  1
    -    0
         1
```

$8041 \div 2 = 4020$ and
remainder 1.

1. Divide and check the answer.

(a)

Dividend = ___
___ × ___ + ___ =

(b)

Dividend = ___
___ × ___ + ___ =

(c)

Dividend = ___
___ × ___ + ___ =

(d)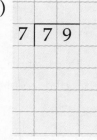

Dividend = ___
___ × ___ + ___ =

Divide.

2. (a)

(b)

(c)

(d)

3. (a) $65 \div 2$ (b) $98 \div 3$ (c) $87 \div 4$ (d) $61 \div 2$ (e) $92 \div 3$

4. (a) $245 \div 2$ (b) $964 \div 3$ (c) $647 \div 2$ (d) $487 \div 4$ (e) $669 \div 6$

5. (a) $207 \div 2$ (b) $308 \div 3$ (c) $809 \div 4$ (d) $504 \div 5$ (e) $703 \div 7$

6. (a) $681 \div 2$ (b) $362 \div 3$ (c) $482 \div 4$ (d) $996 \div 9$ (e) $885 \div 8$

7. (a) $8643 \div 2$ (b) $6967 \div 3$ (c) $4849 \div 4$ (d) $8625 \div 2$ (e) $4887 \div 4$

8. (a) $4025 \div 2$ (b) $9607 \div 3$ (c) $8046 \div 4$ (d) $3605 \div 3$ (e) $2403 \div 2$

9. (a) $8261 \div 2$ (b) $4842 \div 4$ (c) $9632 \div 3$ (d) $6605 \div 6$ (e) $9301 \div 3$

10. (a) $8005 \div 2$ (b) $4007 \div 4$ (c) $3005 \div 3$ (d) $8003 \div 4$ (e) $7004 \div 7$

Do and Learn

Aim To introduce division with regrouping

Things needed Squared paper, scissors, crayons, sheets of paper

Do and Learn

1. Cut strips of squared paper. Each strip should have 10 squares. Colour 2 strips blue and the others pink. Cut squares from the blue strips. A blue square = 1. A pink strip = 10.

2. Show the number 56 with the help of the strips and squares. Then show the division of 56 by 2. To do this, divide the strips and squares between 2 sheets of paper.

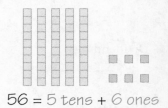

56 = 5 tens + 6 ones

3. First divide the strips (tens) equally between the 2 sheets. Each sheet will get 2 strips, and you will be left with one strip. So, in the division of tens, 1 ten is left over.

```
        T   O
        2
    2 | 5   6
      - 4
        1
```

4. Regroup by exchanging the strip for 10 squares (ones). You will then have 16 ones.

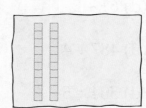  

```
        T   O
        2
    2 | 5   6
      - 4
        1   6
```

5. Divide the squares (ones) equally. Each sheet will have 2 tens and 8 ones, showing the number 28. So, 56 ÷ 2 = 28.

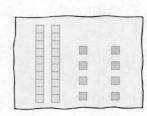 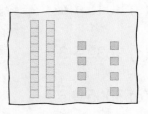

```
        T   O
        2   8
    2 | 5   6
      - 4
        1   6
      - 1   6
        0   0
```

9. More on Division

Division with Regrouping

Divide 56 by 4.

```
      T  O
      1  4
   4│ 5  6
    - 4
      1  6
    - 1  6
      0  0
```

T: $4 \times 2 = 8$.　　$8 > 5$
　 $4 \times 1 = 4$.　　$4 < 5$
　 So, $Q = 1$, $R = 5 - 4 = 1$.
Remainder = 1 ten = 10 ones.
Bring down 6 ones. Together,
10 ones + 6 ones = 16 ones.

O: $16 \div 4 = 4$

∴ $56 \div 4 = 14$.

Divide 79 by 5 and check the answer.

```
      T  O
      1  5
   5│ 7  9
    - 5
      2  9
    - 2  5
      0  4
```

T: $7 \div 5 = ?$
　 $Q = 1$, $R = 7 - 5 = 2$

Remainder = 2 tens = 20 ones.
20 ones + 9 ones = 29 ones.

O: $29 \div 5 = ?$
　 $Q = 5$, $R = 29 - 25 = 4$

$79 \div 5 = 15$ and remainder 4.
$5 \times 15 + 4 = 75 + 4 = 79$ = dividend.
So the answer is correct.

Divide 364 by 5.

```
      H  T  O
         7  2
   5│ 3  6  4
    - 3  5
      0  1  4
       - 1  0
         0  4
```

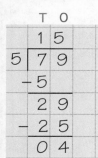

H: $3 < 5$, so $3 \div 5$ ✗
Regroup 3 hundreds and 6 tens
to 36 tens.

T: $36 \div 5 = ?$
　 $Q = 7$, $R = 36 - 35 = 1$

Remainder = 1 ten = 10 ones.
10 ones + 4 ones = 14 ones.

O: $14 \div 5 = ?$
　 $Q = 2$, $R = 14 - 10 = 4$

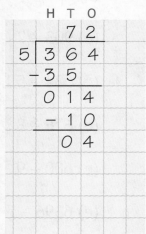

∴ $364 \div 5 = 72$ and remainder 4.

Divide 2413 by 3.

```
      Th H  T  O
            8  0  4
      3│ 2  4  1  3
       - 2  4
         0  0  1
          - 0
            1  3
           - 1  2
            0  1
```

$2413 \div 3 = 804$ and remainder 1.

87

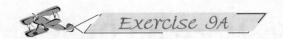

1. Divide and check the answer.

(a)
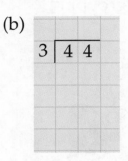

Dividend =
___ × ___ + ___ =

(b)
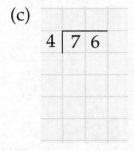

Dividend =
___ × ___ + ___ =

(c)
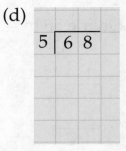

Dividend =
___ × ___ + ___ =

(d)
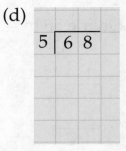

Dividend =
___ × ___ + ___ =

Divide.

2. (a)
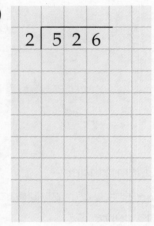

(b)
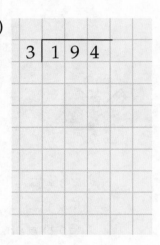

(c)

(d)

3. (a) 42 ÷ 3   (b) 58 ÷ 4   (c) 85 ÷ 5   (d) 91 ÷ 7   (e) 96 ÷ 8

4. (a) 53 ÷ 2   (b) 95 ÷ 4   (c) 67 ÷ 5   (d) 58 ÷ 3   (e) 75 ÷ 6

5. (a) 542 ÷ 2   (b) 789 ÷ 3   (c) 926 ÷ 4   (d) 607 ÷ 5   (e) 903 ÷ 7

6. (a) 560 ÷ 5   (b) 975 ÷ 3   (c) 632 ÷ 6   (d) 816 ÷ 8   (e) 534 ÷ 5

7. (a) 637 ÷ 7   (b) 135 ÷ 2   (c) 195 ÷ 3   (d) 326 ÷ 5   (e) 676 ÷ 8

8. (a) 923 ÷ 4   (b) 604 ÷ 5   (c) 245 ÷ 6   (d) 960 ÷ 8   (e) 600 ÷ 9

9. (a) 5514 ÷ 6   (b) 4842 ÷ 5   (c) 2181 ÷ 3   (d) 3575 ÷ 5   (e) 6396 ÷ 7

10. (a) 4216 ÷ 6   (b) 7256 ÷ 8   (c) 8181 ÷ 9   (d) 6804 ÷ 8   (e) 4850 ÷ 5

More sums for practice

11. (a) 90 ÷ 5   (b) 96 ÷ 6   (c) 75 ÷ 4   (d) 89 ÷ 7

12. (a) 608 ÷ 4   (b) 712 ÷ 2   (c) 857 ÷ 5   (d) 954 ÷ 8

13. (a) 854 ÷ 2   (b) 675 ÷ 6   (c) 418 ÷ 4   (d) 872 ÷ 8

14. (a) 469 ÷ 7   (b) 308 ÷ 5   (c) 540 ÷ 6   (d) 212 ÷ 3

15. (a) 7348 ÷ 4   (b) 2718 ÷ 3   (c) 8165 ÷ 8   (d) 3015 ÷ 3

Division by 10, 100 and 1000

Divide 69, 457 and 2368 by 10.

```
        6
  10 | 6 9
     -6 0
        9
```
Q = 6,
R = 9

```
       4 5
  10 | 4 5 7
     -4 0
       0 5 7
       - 5 0
         0 7
```
Q = 45, R = 7

```
       2 3 6
  10 | 2 3 6 8
     -2 0
       0 3 6
       -3 0
         0 6 8
         -0 6 0
             0 8
```
Q = 236, R = 8

Divide 720 and 3795 by 100.

720 = 700 + 20
As 7 x 100 = 700, 700 ÷ 100 = 7.
20 ÷ 100 ✗. So, R = 20.
∴ 720 ÷ 100 = 7 and remainder 20.

3795 = 3700 + 95
As 37 x 100 = 3700, 3700 ÷ 100 = 37.
95 ÷ 100 ✗. So, R = 95.
∴ 3795 ÷ 100 = 37 and remainder 95.

Divide 4630 by 1000.

4630 = 4000 + 630
As 4 x 1000 = 4000, 4000 ÷ 1000 = 4.
630 ÷ 1000 ✗. So, R = 630.
∴ 4630 ÷ 1000 = 4 and remainder 630.

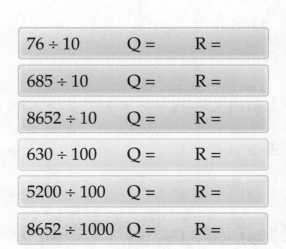

The zeros in the divisor (10, 100, or 1000) help in getting the answer.
256⁷ ÷ 1̲0̲   Q = 256, R = 7
25̲6̲7̲ ÷ 1̲0̲0̲   Q = 25, R = 67
25̲6̲7̲ ÷ 1̲0̲0̲0̲   Q = 2, R = 567

Do these quickly.

47 ÷ 10	Q =	R =	76 ÷ 10	Q =	R =
332 ÷ 10	Q =	R =	685 ÷ 10	Q =	R =
1256 ÷ 10	Q =	R =	8652 ÷ 10	Q =	R =
564 ÷ 100	Q =	R =	630 ÷ 100	Q =	R =
1345 ÷ 100	Q =	R =	5200 ÷ 100	Q =	R =
5379 ÷ 1000	Q =	R =	8652 ÷ 1000	Q =	R =

Division by a 2-digit Number

> The first digit of the dividend will be always less than the 2-digit divisor. So, start with the first two digits of the dividend.

Divide 385 by 12.

```
      H T O
          3 2
  1 2 | 3 8 5
      - 3 6
        0 2 5
        - 2 4
          0 1
```

T: 12 × 4 = 48.   48 > 38
   12 × 3 = 36.   36 < 38
   So, Q = 3, R = 38 − 36 = 2.
   Remainder = 2 tens = 20 ones.
   Bring down 5 ones. Together,
   20 ones + 5 ones = 25 ones.
   O: 25 ÷ 12 = 2, R = 1

∴ 385 ÷ 12 = 32 and remainder 1.

Divide 129 by 13.

```
      H T O
            9
  1 3 | 1 2 9
      - 1 1 7
        0 1 2
```

12 < 13
So divide by taking
3 digits of the
dividend.

∴ 129 ÷ 13 = 9 and remainder 12.

Exercise 9B

Divide.

1. (a) 111 ÷ 11   (b) 121 ÷ 11   (c) 495 ÷ 11   (d) 109 ÷ 11

2. (a) 132 ÷ 12   (b) 489 ÷ 12   (c) 384 ÷ 12   (d) 110 ÷ 12

3. (a) 143 ÷ 13   (b) 556 ÷ 13   (c) 395 ÷ 13   (d) 125 ÷ 13

4. (a) 154 ÷ 14   (b) 284 ÷ 14   (c) 728 ÷ 14   (d) 133 ÷ 14

5. (a) 300 ÷ 15   (b) 165 ÷ 15   (c) 497 ÷ 15   (d) 126 ÷ 15

1. A bus has 8 rows of seats. Each row has equal number of seats. If 48 children can sit in the bus, how many seats are there in each row?

```
      6
  8 | 4 8
    − 4 8
      0 0
```

There are 6 seats in each row.

2. 112 pencils were divided equally among 9 children. How many pencils did each child get? How many pencils were left?

```
        1 2
  9 | 1 1 2
    −  9
        2 2
      − 1 8
        0 4
```

Each child got 12 pencils.
4 pencils were left.

3.  Tom stuck 76 photos in his album. If he stuck 4 photos on each page, how many pages did he use?

4. Mou can cut 7 pieces out of one cake. How many cakes does she need for 84 guests?

5. 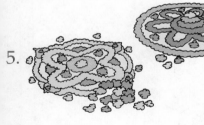 127 flowers were divided equally to make 8 rangolis. How many flowers were used for each? How many flowers were left?

6. Do these sums in your notebook.

   (a) If 144 books are placed equally on 12 shelves, how many are there on each shelf?

   (b) If 6 glasses are packed in a box, how many boxes are needed for 84 glasses?

   (c) Sri needs 315 earthen lamps to decorate his house. The lamps come in boxes of 15. How many boxes should he buy?

   (d) Achin arranged 100 flowers equally in 8 vases. How many flowers went into each vase? How many flowers were left?

Even and Odd Numbers

Numbers that leave no remainder on being divided by 2 are called even numbers.

0, 2, 4, 6 and 8 are even 1-digit numbers. They are called even digits.
Some more even numbers: 12, 24, 64, 36, 276, 50, 1310, 108 and 9678.

$$\begin{array}{r} 3\ 5 \\ 2\overline{\smash{)}7\ 0} \\ -6 \\ \hline 1\ 0 \\ 1\ 0 \\ \hline 0\ 0 \end{array}$$

∴ 70 is even.

Numbers that leave a remainder on being divided by 2 are called odd numbers.

(Numbers that are not even are odd numbers.)
1, 3, 5, 7 and 9 are odd 1-digit numbers. They are called odd digits.
Some more odd numbers: 11, 41, 163, 35, 485, 57, 2227, 89 and 8769.

$$\begin{array}{r} 4 \\ 2\overline{\smash{)}9} \\ -8 \\ \hline 1 \end{array}$$

∴ 9 is odd.

> An even number has an even digit at ones place.
> An odd number has an odd digit at ones place.

Look at the numbers in the triangle.
Do you see a pattern?
(A number in a white 'cell' is the sum of the two numbers above it.)
Now spot the even numbers.
Colour their cells pink.
Do you see a pattern?
Spot the first twenty odd numbers from the top. (Leave out the 1s.)
Colour their cells yellow.

```
                        1
                     1     1
                  1     2     1
               1     3     3     1
            1     4     6     4     1
         1     5    10    10     5     1
      1     6    15    20    15     6     1
   1     7    21    35    35    21     7     1
1     8    28    56    70    56    28     8     1
1  9   36   84  126  126   84   36    9    1
1  10  45  120 210 252 210 120  45  10   1
1 11  55  165 330 462 462 330 165  55  11  1
1 12  66 220 495 792 924 792 495 220 66 12  1
1 13 78 286 715 1287 1716 1716 1287 715 286 78 13 1
1 14 91 364 1001 2002 3003 3432 3003 2002 1001 364 91 14 1
```

Review Worksheet 3

Multiply.

1. (a)
$$\begin{array}{r} 3\ 5 \\ \times\ \ \ 2 \\ \hline \end{array}$$

(b)
$$\begin{array}{r} 4\ 7 \\ \times\ \ \ 7 \\ \hline \end{array}$$

(c)
$$\begin{array}{r} 1\ 2\ 4 \\ \times\ \ \ \ \ 3 \\ \hline \end{array}$$

(d)
$$\begin{array}{r} 7\ 0\ 8 \\ \times\ \ \ \ \ 6 \\ \hline \end{array}$$

(e)
$$\begin{array}{r} 4\ 8\ 3 \\ \times\ \ \ \ \ 9 \\ \hline \end{array}$$

2. (a)
$$\begin{array}{r} 2\ 4 \\ \times\ 6\ 0 \\ \hline \end{array}$$

(b)
$$\begin{array}{r} 5\ 2 \\ \times\ 7\ 0 \\ \hline \end{array}$$

(c)
$$\begin{array}{r} 1\ 7\ 5 \\ \times\ \ 3\ 0 \\ \hline \end{array}$$

(d)
$$\begin{array}{r} 2\ 0\ 7 \\ \times\ \ 9\ 0 \\ \hline \end{array}$$

(e)
$$\begin{array}{r} 2\ 6 \\ \times\ 3\ 0\ 0 \\ \hline \end{array}$$

3. (a)
$$\begin{array}{r} 3\ 2 \\ \times\ 4\ 8 \\ \hline \end{array}$$

(b)
$$\begin{array}{r} 6\ 4 \\ \times\ 7\ 5 \\ \hline \end{array}$$

(c)
$$\begin{array}{r} 1\ 2\ 7 \\ \times\ \ 2\ 3 \\ \hline \end{array}$$

(d)
$$\begin{array}{r} 2\ 2\ 1 \\ \times\ \ 3\ 6 \\ \hline \end{array}$$

(e)
$$\begin{array}{r} 3\ 2\ 1 \\ \times\ \ 2\ 7 \\ \hline \end{array}$$

4. Divide and check the answer.

(a) $2\,|\,3\ 9$

(b) $4\,|\,7\ 5$

(c) $12\,|\,4\ 8$

(d) $15\,|\,6\ 1$

Dividend =
___ × ___ + ___ =

Dividend =
___ × ___ + ___ =

Dividend =
___ × ___ + ___ =

Dividend =
___ × ___ + ___ =

5. Divide.

(a) $3\,|\,1\ 9\ 8$

(b) $7\,|\,7\ 2\ 3$

(c) $5\,|\,3\ 4\ 0\ 3$

(d) $9\,|\,3\ 6\ 8\ 9$

MathGym

Do you know your multiplication tables? Fill in as shown.

×	1	2	3	4	5	6	7	8	9	10	11	12	13	14	15
1		2				6							13		
2		4				12							26		
3		6				18							39		
4		8				24							52		
5		10				30							65		
6		12				36							78		
7		14				42							91		
8		16				48							104		
9		18				54							117		
10		20				60							130		

Find the pattern and fill in.

13	➡	39	56	➡	8	24	➡	2400	54	➡	9
14	➡	42	63	➡	9	3	➡	300	12	➡	2
12	➡		77	➡		5	➡		108	➡	

Join the numbers that can be divided by 7. (You can only join a number with another in the next row.) Which Roman numeral does the shape remind you of?

16	14	13	21	17
30	32	35	37	39
40	42	52	84	72

Do and Learn

Aim To understand fractions

Things needed Equal-sized strips of paper, colour pencils, sticks/toothpicks

Do and Learn

1. Divide 6 sticks equally between 2 of your friends.
   Each friend will get 3 sticks.

2. Now try dividing 7 sticks equally between them.
   After your friends get 3 sticks each, 1 stick will
   be left. To divide the stick equally, break it into
   two equal parts.
   Each part is half of the stick.
   Half is 1 part out of 2 equal parts.
   It is written as $\frac{1}{2}$.

3. Fold a strip of paper as shown. Then open it out.
   The fold divides the strip into two equal parts.
   Each part is half of the strip.

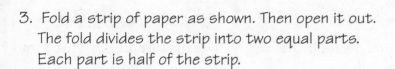

4. Colour one part. Now half the strip is coloured.
   Colour the other half. The whole strip is coloured.
   So, two halves make a whole.

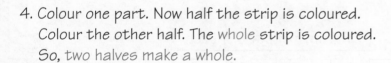

5. Fold a strip of paper in half. Fold it again in half.
   Then open it out. The folds divide the paper into 4
   equal parts. Each part is one fourth of the whole.
   One fourth is written as $\frac{1}{4}$. Four one fourths make
   a whole.

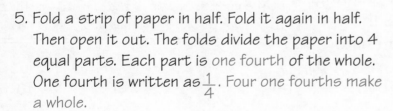

6. Colour 2 parts out of four. Now two one fourths or
   two fourths ($\frac{2}{4}$) are coloured. Also colour half of
   an equal-sized strip. You will find that the coloured
   areas are equal in both the strips.
   So, 2 parts out of 4 = 1 part out of 2
   $$\frac{2}{4} = \frac{1}{2}.$$

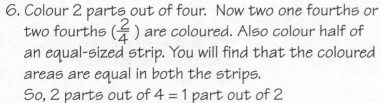

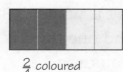
$\frac{2}{4}$ coloured

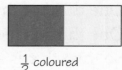
$\frac{1}{2}$ coloured

95

10. Fractions

When a thing is divided into equal parts, each part is called a fraction of the whole (the full thing).

Suppose a cake is divided into 6 equal parts. Each part is one sixth of the whole cake.

One sixth is a fraction (or fractional number). It is written as $\frac{1}{6}$.

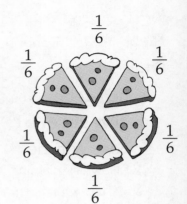

Half

When something is divided into two equal parts, each part is one half of the whole. One half is written as $\frac{1}{2}$.

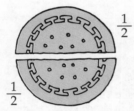

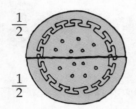

The biscuit is divided into 2 equal parts. Each part is one half of the whole biscuit.

The two halves make the whole biscuit.

half + half = whole (one)

This biscuit is divided into 2 unequal parts.

The parts are not halves.

To write a fraction in numbers, we write $\dfrac{\text{number of parts chosen}}{\text{total number of equal parts}}$.

 In one part out of 2 is chosen by shading. We say $\frac{1}{2}$ is shaded. In $\frac{1}{2}$, 1 is the numerator and 2 is the denominator.

The number on top is the numerator. The number at the bottom is the denominator.

One Third

When something is divided into three equal parts, each part is one third ($\frac{1}{3}$) of the whole. Two one thirds together make two thirds ($\frac{2}{3}$). Three one thirds together make the whole.

One third of this flag is white.
One third is red. And one third is blue.
So, two thirds are coloured.
The three one thirds together make the whole flag.

3 one thirds = whole(1).

96

One Fourth

When something is divided into four equal parts, each part is one fourth ($\frac{1}{4}$) of the whole. One fourth is also called a quarter.

Raju, Sania, Mira and Neel shared a pizza equally.

So, each got one fourth of it.

The girls got one half of the pizza.

The boys got the other half.

So, two one fourths make half.

Raju, Mira and Neel ate their shares. So, three fourths ($\frac{3}{4}$) of the pizza was over.

Sania took her share ($\frac{1}{4}$) home.

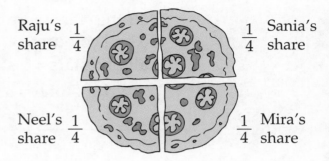

Raju's share $\frac{1}{4}$ $\frac{1}{4}$ Sania's share

Neel's share $\frac{1}{4}$ $\frac{1}{4}$ Mira's share

2 one fourths = half
3 one fourths = three fourths
4 one fourths = whole

Some More Fractions

Here are some more examples of fractions. The coloured parts show the fractions.

 $\frac{1}{5}$

 $\frac{3}{4}$

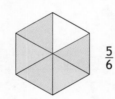 $\frac{5}{6}$

$\frac{3}{7}$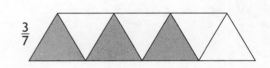

$\frac{1}{6}$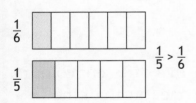
$\frac{1}{5}$
$\frac{1}{5} > \frac{1}{6}$

$\frac{3}{6}$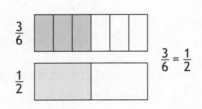
$\frac{1}{2}$
$\frac{3}{6} = \frac{1}{2}$

Fraction name follows the ordinal name of the denominator.

$\frac{1}{5}$ = one fifth $\frac{3}{5}$ = three fifths

$\frac{1}{9}$ = one ninth $\frac{5}{9}$ = five ninths

$\frac{1}{10}$ = one tenth $\frac{6}{10}$ = six tenths

 Whole

 $\frac{1}{2}$ $\frac{1}{2}$

 $\frac{1}{2}$ $\frac{1}{2}$

 $\frac{1}{2}$ $\frac{1}{2}$

There can be many ways in which a whole can be divided into equal parts.

 $\frac{1}{4}$ $\frac{1}{4}$ $\frac{1}{4}$ $\frac{1}{4}$

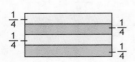 $\frac{1}{4}$ $\frac{1}{4}$ $\frac{1}{4}$ $\frac{1}{4}$

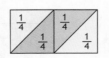 $\frac{1}{4}$ $\frac{1}{4}$ $\frac{1}{4}$ $\frac{1}{4}$

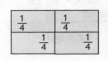 $\frac{1}{4}$ $\frac{1}{4}$ $\frac{1}{4}$ $\frac{1}{4}$

Fractions in Collections

Raj had a collection (group) of 6 stars.
He coloured every other star in the group.
Half the stars were coloured.
He had coloured 3.
Half of 6 stars = 3 stars. $6 \div 2$ is also 3.
We write $\frac{1}{2}$ of 6 = 3.

To find half of a number, divide by 2.

$\frac{1}{2}$ of 4 = 2 $\frac{1}{2}$ of 8 = 4 $\frac{1}{2}$ of 12 = 6

3 children made hand prints on a T-shirt.
The whole design had 15 fingers.
Each hand print (5 fingers) was one third of the design.
So, one third of 15 is 5. $15 \div 3$ is also 5.
We write $\frac{1}{3}$ of 15 = 5.

To find a third, divide by 3.

$\frac{1}{3}$ of 6 = 2 $\frac{1}{3}$ of 9 = 3 $\frac{1}{3}$ of 12 = 4

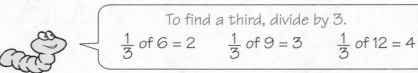

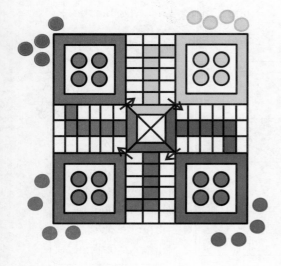

The 16 counters in Ludo come in 4 different colours.
The 4 counters of a colour are one fourth of the 16 counters.
So, one fourth of 16 is 4. $16 \div 4$ is also 4.
We write $\frac{1}{4}$ of 16 = 4.

To find a fourth, divide by 4.

$\frac{1}{4}$ of 8 = 2 $\frac{1}{4}$ of 12 = 3 $\frac{1}{4}$ of 20 = 5

Tick the figures that show halves.

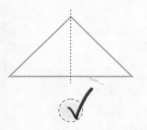 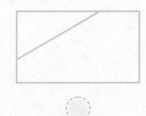  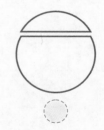

Colour to show the fractions.

   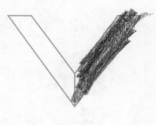

$\frac{1}{3}$
   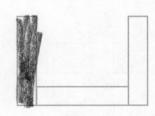

$\frac{1}{4}$
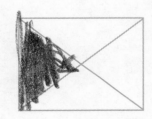  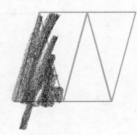 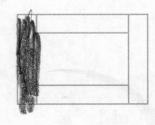

Write 'T' for true and 'F' for false.

One third is coloured. T

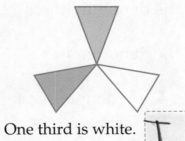
One third is white. T

A quarter is white. T

Colour to show the fractions.

What fraction is shaded?

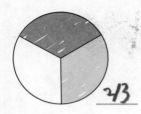 2/3
 2/4
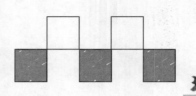 3/5
 2/6

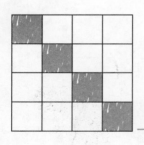 4/12
 6/8
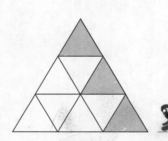 3/9
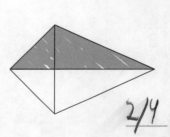 2/4

Fill in.

$\frac{1}{2}$ of 4 = **2** $\frac{1}{2}$ of 12 = **6** $\frac{1}{3}$ of 9 = **3** $\frac{1}{5}$ of 10 = **2** $\frac{1}{9}$ of 18 = **2**

One third of 18 = **6**   A quarter of 16 = **4**   One sixth of 24 = **4**

In $\frac{3}{4}$ the numerator is **3** and the denominator is **4**.

In $\frac{7}{9}$ the numerator is **7** and the denominator is **9**.

The fraction whose numerator is 4 and denominator is 7 is **4/7**.

The fraction whose numerator is 11 and denominator is 13 is **11/13**

Colour two thirds of the collection of stars.

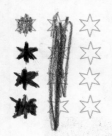 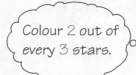 

Colour 2 out of every 3 stars.

Or
How many 3s in 12 stars?
12 ÷ 3 = 4.
Colour 2 × 4 = 8 stars.

Exercise 10B

Colour to show the fractions.

$\frac{1}{5}$  $\frac{3}{7}$  $\frac{2}{6}$  $\frac{5}{8}$

$\frac{4}{10}$

Colour the fractions, count and write.

$\frac{1}{2}$ of 6 = 3

$\frac{2}{3}$ of 6 = 1

$\frac{3}{4}$ of 8 = $\frac{6}{8}$

$\frac{2}{3}$ of 9 = $\frac{6}{9}$

$\frac{3}{4}$ of 12 = $\frac{9}{12}$

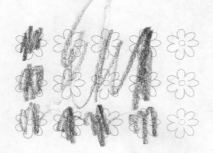

$\frac{4}{5}$ of 15 = $\frac{12}{15}$

$\frac{5}{6}$ of 18 = $\frac{15}{18}$

Tick if the fractions are shaded correctly.

$\frac{1}{3}$ 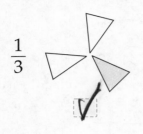 ✓

$\frac{1}{3}$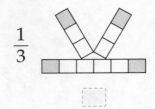

$\frac{2}{3}$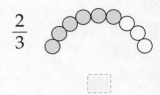

$\frac{3}{4}$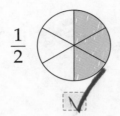

$\frac{1}{2}$ 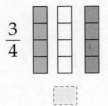 ✓

$\frac{3}{4}$

$\frac{1}{2}$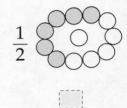

$\frac{1}{4}$ 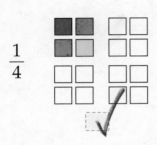 ✓

$\frac{2}{3}$

$\frac{2}{5}$

Shade to show the two fractions and then write <, > or =.

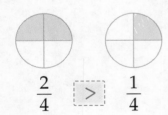

$\frac{2}{4}$ $>$ $\frac{1}{4}$

$\frac{1}{3}$ $>$ $\frac{2}{3}$

$\frac{2}{7}$ $<$ $\frac{4}{7}$

$\frac{1}{3}$ $>$ $\frac{1}{4}$

$\frac{1}{3}$ $<$ $\frac{1}{2}$

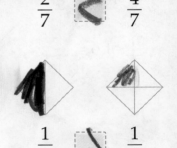

$\frac{1}{2}$ $>$ $\frac{1}{4}$

$\frac{2}{3}$ $>$ $\frac{1}{2}$

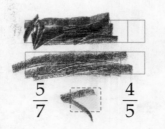

$\frac{5}{7}$ $<$ $\frac{4}{5}$

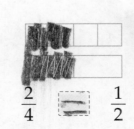

$\frac{2}{4}$ $=$ $\frac{1}{2}$

$\frac{3}{4}$ $<$ $\frac{2}{3}$

102

Nine children went for a picnic. If one third of them were girls, how many boys were there?

$9 \div 3 = 3.$
$\therefore \frac{1}{3}$ of $9 = 3.$
So, the number of girls = 3.
$\therefore$ the number of boys $= 9 - 3 = 6.$

Ajay read one fifth of a 100-page book. How many pages of the book did he read?

20

An hour has 60 minutes. How many minutes is a quarter of an hour?

15

Ali shared 1 litre of pineapple juice equally with three friends. How much did each friend get?

Eight children shared a pizza equally. What fraction of the pizza did each child get?

$\frac{1}{8}$

Jyothi had 24 sweets. She gave one third of them to Vijaya. How many sweets were left?

16

Swati has watered one fourth of her plants. If she has 16 plants, how many more plants does she have to water?

11. Lines and Shapes

Look at a sheet of paper. Its sides meet at corners. The sides have some length, which you can measure with a ruler. But the corners have no length. They are just the place (position) where the sides meet. The corners are points.

A point gives a position.

A point does not have length or thickness. To show a point on a sheet of paper, press the tip of a pencil on it. Mark a few points. Name them A, B, C, O, P, X, Y, and so on. These points show different positions on the sheet.

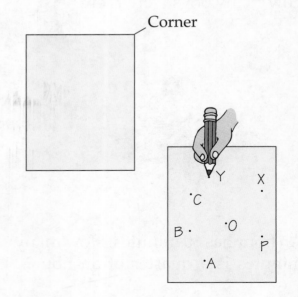
Corner

Lines

When the tip of your pencil moves across paper, it moves along a line.
The line can be straight or curved.
Straight lines can be horizontal, vertical or slanting.

Horizontal line   Vertical line   Slanting lines   Curved lines

Line segment

Look at the points A and B. A straight line can pass through them. But only a part of the line will lie between A and B.

The part of a straight line between two points is called a line segment. (Segment means a part.)

So, between A and B we have the line segment AB.

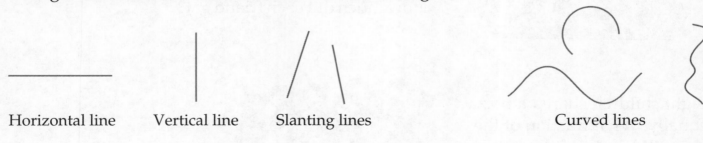
A   B

Let us draw a line segment between two points .
Place a ruler touching the points O and P. Run the pencil along the ruler, from one point to the other. You will get the line segment OP.

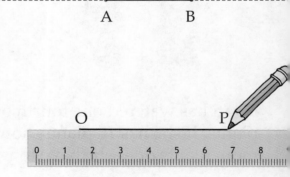
O   P

Remember that only one straight line can pass through two points. But there can be many curved lines between two points.

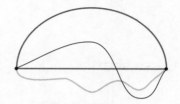

Lines and Shapes

Draw a curved line between two points A and B. Then continue the line by moving the pencil from B to A along a different path. You will get a closed shape.

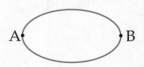

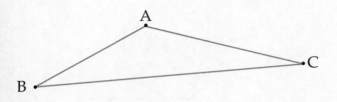

You cannot make a closed shape with just one straight line. You need at least three straight lines to draw a closed shape with straight sides. The line segments AB, BC and CA form the triangle ABC.

Trace over the curved lines and name the shapes.

Draw straight lines between the dots of the same colour to get closed shapes. Name the shapes you get.

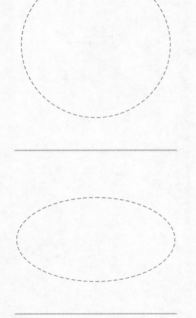

Flat Shapes

You know these shapes.

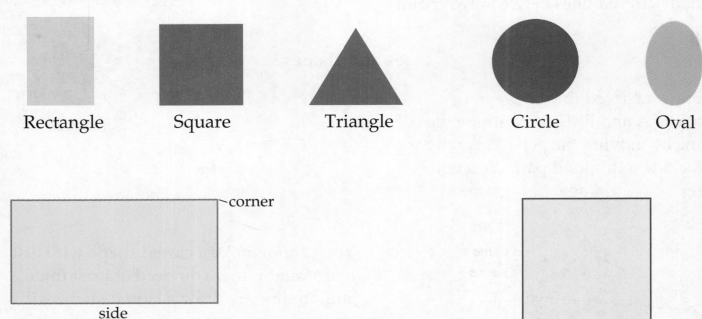

Rectangle   Square   Triangle   Circle   Oval

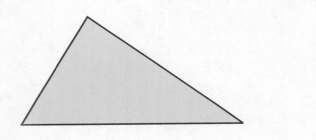

A rectangle has 4 sides and 4 corners. Its opposite sides are equal.

A square has 4 sides and 4 corners. All sides of a square are equal.

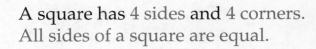

number of sides = number of corners
Figures with no corners have no sides.

A triangle has 3 sides and 3 corners.

Circles and ovals have no sides and no corners.

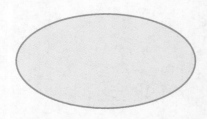

Do and Learn

Aim To learn about the sizes of the faces and edges of cubes and cuboids

Things needed Dice/magic cube, matchbox, sheets of paper, pencil

Do and Learn

1. Trace the outline of any of the faces of a dice
   or a magic cube. Is the outline a square?
   Place the other faces on the outline.
   Are all the faces of the same size?
   Are all the edges of the same size?

2. Do the same with a matchbox.
   Is the outline a square or a rectangle?
   Are all the faces of the same size?
   Are all the edges of the same size?

Cube

A dice is a cube.

When you roll a dice, you want the face with six to
come up. Solid shapes have flat or curved faces
(surfaces). A cube has 6 flat faces.

The faces meet at edges. A cube has 12 equal edges.

The edges meet at corners. A cube has 8 corners.

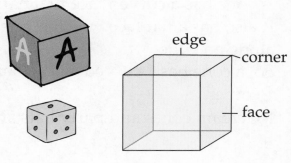

Cube

Cuboid

Matchboxes, bricks, rooms and cupboards
are cuboids.

Like a cube, a cuboid has 6 flat faces.

A cuboid has 12 edges and 8 corners.

All the edges of a cuboid are not equal.

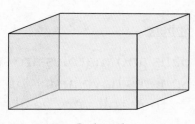

Cuboid

Some things have a curved face (surface).
A curved face helps in rolling.
You can make a battery roll on its curved face,
but not on its flat face.

Cylinder

A rolling pin has a curved face, which we use to
make rotis. It also has two flat faces to which the
handles are stuck.

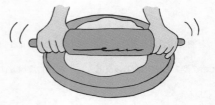

Rolling pins and batteries are cylinders.
A cylinder has 1 curved face and 2 flat faces.
Each flat face meets the curved face along an edge.
So, a cylinder has 2 edges.
It has no corners.

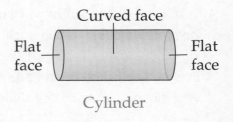

Cone

A cone has a curved face that narrows to a corner.
It also has a flat face which meets the curved face
along an edge.
So, a cone has 1 curved face, 1 flat face, 1 edge and
1 corner.
Ice cream cones and party hats are conical.

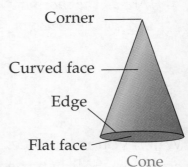

Sphere

Balls and marbles are spheres.
Spheres have just 1 curved face.
So they roll very easily.
There are no edges, corners or flat
faces to stop them from rolling.

Sphere

Name all the line segments in each shape.

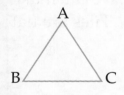  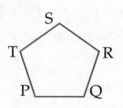 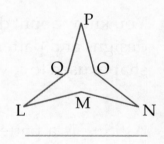

_____ _____ _____ _____

_____ _____ _____ _____

How many corners, how many sides?

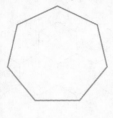  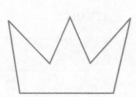 

_____ _____ _____ _____

_____ _____ _____ _____

Fill in.

In a rectangle, the _____ sides are equal.

A circle has _____ sides and _____ corners.

A cube has _____ faces and _____ edges.

A sphere has 1 _____ face.

A cylinder has _____ flat faces, _____ curved face, and _____ edges.

A cone has _____ curved face and _____ flat face.

Write 'T' for true and 'F' for false.

The part of a line between two points is called a line segment. _____

An oval has just one side. _____

All the edges of a cuboid are equal. _____

All the edges of a cube are equal. _____

You can draw many straight lines through two points. _____

12. Shapes and Designs

You know about different flat shapes. By repeating some of these shapes, we can make designs and patterns. You must have seen such designs made with tiles. Tiles are flat shapes used to cover a surface.

Tiling

A tiling is a pattern. It is made of shapes fitting neatly next to each other, without leaving gaps. Here are some examples of tiling. They are made with shapes that have equal sides.

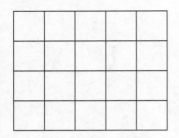 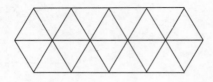 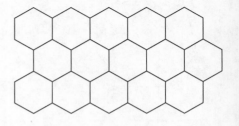

Tiling with a square

Tiling with a triangle that has equal sides

Tiling with a 6-sided shape with equal sides

You can use tiles of two different colours to make different patterns.

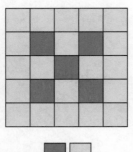 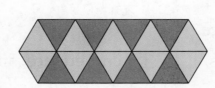 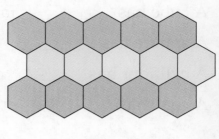

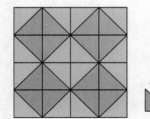   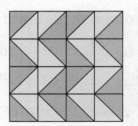

Count the number of tiles in a row and find the number of tiles.

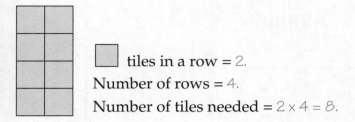

tiles in a row = 2.
Number of rows = 4.
Number of tiles needed = 2 × 4 = 8.

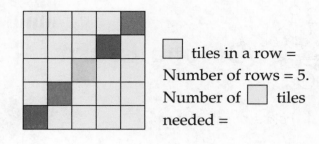

☐ tiles in a row =
Number of rows = 5.
Number of ☐ tiles
needed =

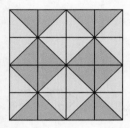

◺ + ◿ tiles in a row =
Number of rows = 4.
Number of tiles needed =

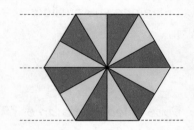

Yellow tiles in a row =
Number of rows = 2.
Number of yellow tiles
needed =

Complete the patterns.

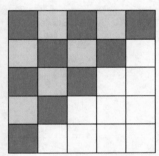

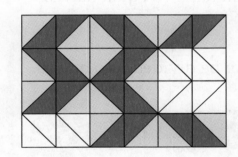

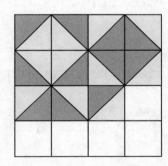

Divide the squares into four triangles, as shown.
Colour the triangles to make your own pattern.

111

Shapes That Have Halves

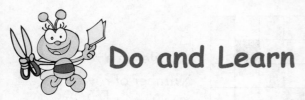

Do and Learn

1. Fold a sheet of paper.

2. Draw this shape and cut along the outline, along the path shown.

End

Start →

3. Open out the shape. Does it look like a dress? This is how tailors cut out clothes. They can do this because our body has two equal halves.

Most animals have a body that has two equal halves.

Here are some shapes that can be divided into halves.

  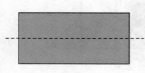   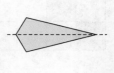

Draw a line to divide the shapes into halves.

112

Tangram

Tangram is an old Chinese game of shapes. It has 7 pieces called tans. You can make different shapes with these pieces.

Trace this shape on chart paper. Cut along the lines to get 7 pieces.

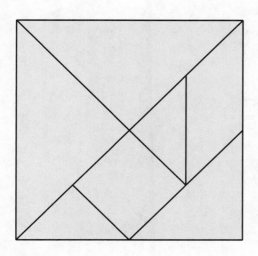 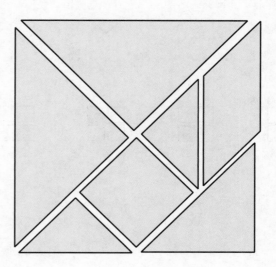

Use the large triangles to make a square.

Use the small triangles to make a triangle.

Use three triangles to make a house.

Make a tree.

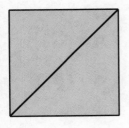 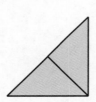 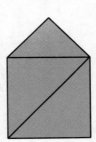 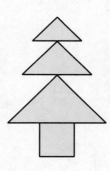

Make a boat.

Make a cat.

Make a rabbit.

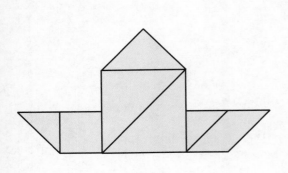  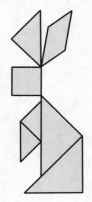

13. Patterns

Continue the pattern.

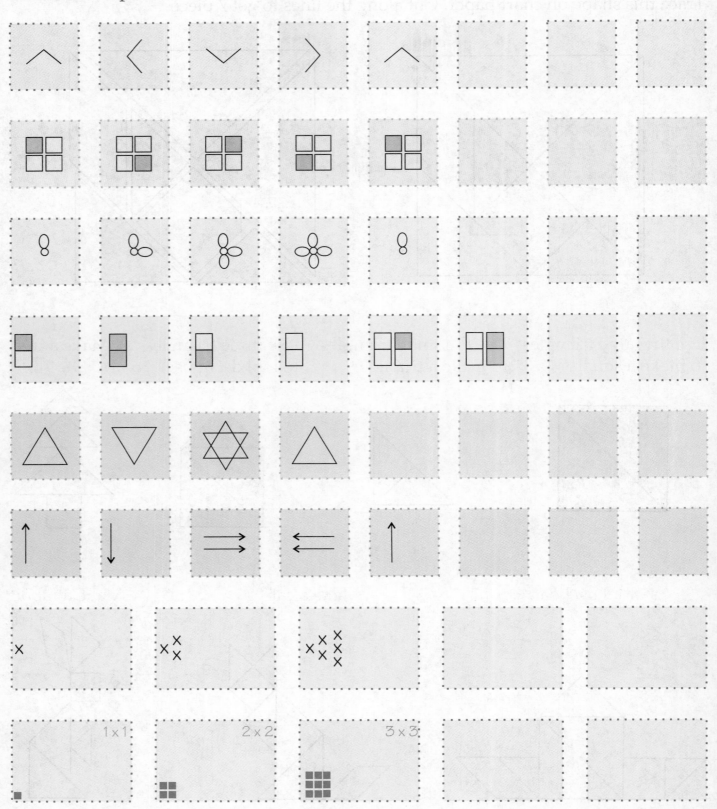

Continue the pattern.

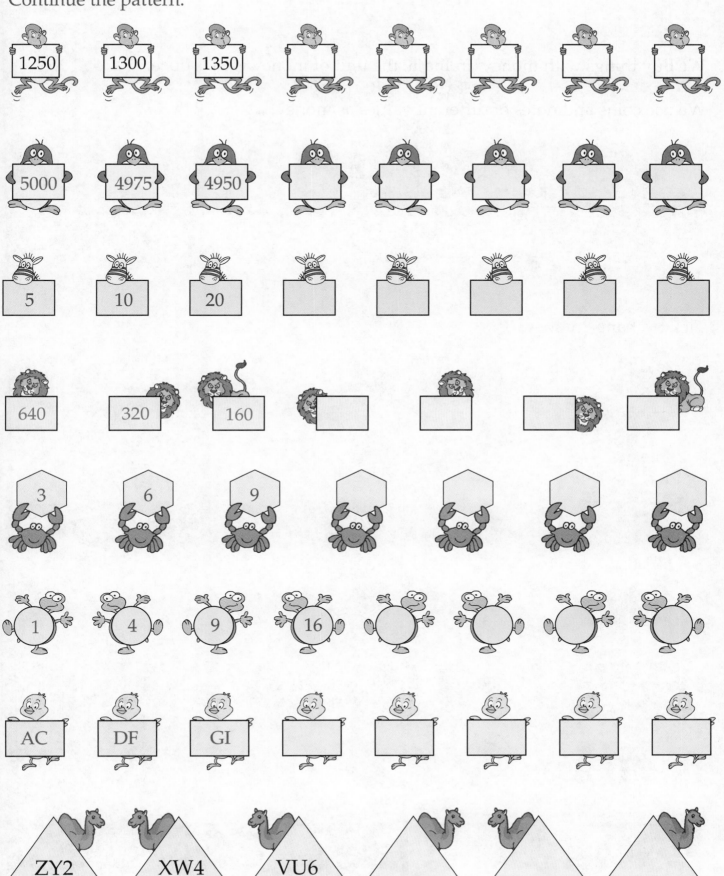

1250 1300 1350

5000 4975 4950

5 10 20

640 320 160

3 6 9

1 4 9 16

AC DF GI

ZY2 XW4 VU6

115

14. Money

We buy things with money. In India, the unit of money is the rupee.

1 rupee = 100 paise.

We use coins and notes of different values as money.

Tick to change money.

We use the short forms Re for rupee, Rs for rupees and p for paise.
₹ too means rupee or rupees.

　　1 rupee = Re 1 or ₹ 1　　　　15 rupees = Rs 15 or ₹ 15　　　　50 paise = 50 p

Also, 168 rupees = Rs 168.00　　　50 paise = Re 0.50

　　60 rupees and 50 paise together = Rs 60.50
　　　　(In words: sixty rupees fifty paise)

Rupees are to the left of the point (.), and paise are to its right.

How much money?

Re 0.50　　　　_____　　　_____　　　_____

_____　　_____　　_____　　_____

Changing Rupees to Paise, Paise to Rupees

Rs 2 = Re 1 + Re 1 = 2 × Re 1
　　　= 2 × 100 p = 200 p

₹ 10 = 10 × 100 p = 1000 p

Rs 7.50 = Rs 7 + 50 p
　　　　= 700 p + 50 p = 750 p

Short cuts
To change rupees to paise, put two zeros at the end of the number.

To change Rs and p to paise, write the numbers together, without the point.

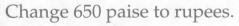

Change 650 paise to rupees.

1 rupee = 100 paise.
To find how many rupees in 650 p, divide by 100 p.
650 ÷ 100 = 6 and remainder 50.
So, 650 p = Rs 6 and 50 p = Rs 6.50.

To change paise to rupees, place a point after two digits from the right.

1065 p = Rs 10.65　　　　2600 p = Rs 26.00　　　　45 p = Re 0.45　　　　5 p = Re 0.05

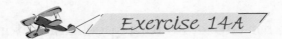

1. Change to paise.

(a) Rs 5 = _____   (b) Rs 68 = _____   (c) Rs 90 = _____

(d) Rs 8.50 = _____   (e) ₹ 11.00 = _____   (f) ₹ 87.75 = _____

2. Change to rupees.

(a) 3225 p = _____   (b) 265 p = _____   (c) 50 p = _____   (d) 8 p = _____

(e) 2700 p = _____   (f) 45325 p = _____   (g) 67215 p = _____

3. Fill in the blanks.

(a) Rs 7.10 = _____ p   (b) ₹ 25 = _____ p   (c) Rs 76.00 = _____ p

(d) 5000 p = Rs_____   (e) 4995 p = ₹_____   (f) 6845 p = Rs_____

Addition and Subtraction of Money

To add or subtract money, write the rupees and paise in separate columns or with a point between them. Then add or subtract like ordinary numbers. If you use points to separate the rupees and paise, put the point in the answer too.

Find Rs 142.65 + Rs 23.50 + Rs 10.

```
  Rs      p
     1
  1 4 2  6 5
+   2 3  5 0
+   1 0  0 0
  1 7 6  1 5
```

First add the paise.
65 p + 50 p + 0 p = 115 p = Re 1 + 15 p
Write 15 under paise. Carry Re 1 to the ones place of rupees. Add the rupees.

```
        1
Rs 1 4 2 . 6 5
+ Rs   2 3 . 5 0
+ Rs   1 0 . 0 0
Rs 1 7 6 . 1 5
```

Answer: Rs 176.15

Find Rs 8.25 – Rs 5.50.

```
  Rs      p
   7   1 2 5
   8   2 5
-  5   5 0
   2   7 5
```

25 p – 50 p ✗   So, borrow Re 1 (100 p) from Rs 8. Regroup Rs 8 and 25 p as Rs 7 and 125 p, and subtract.

Answer: Rs 2.75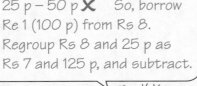

You may subtract like ordinary numbers, as shown here.

```
        7  12
₹  8 . 2 5
- ₹ 5 . 5 0
₹  2 . 7 5
```

Add.

1. (a)
Rs   p

| | 2 0 |
| + | 4 0 |

(b)
Rs   p

| | 5 0 |
| + | 7 5 |

(c)
Rs   p

| | 6 0 |
| + | 2 0 |

(d)
Rs   p

| | 1 3 | 4 5 |
| + | 2 4 | 2 5 |

(e)
Rs   p

| | 2 5 | 7 0 |
| + | 8 2 | 5 0 |

2. (a)
Rs 20.55
+ Rs 340.30

(b)
Rs 271.60
+ Rs 432.40

(c)
₹ 501.75
+ ₹ 128.50

(d)
₹ 434.50
+ ₹ 626.50

3. (a)
    Rs 1123.45
  + Rs 2356.45

(b) Rs 107.35
  + Rs   67.20
  + Rs 115.25

(c) Rs 271.55
  + Rs 386.25
  + Rs 168.30

(d) Rs 1427.25
  + Rs 3846.25
  + Rs 2628.50

4. (a) Rs 96.35 + Rs 37.85   (b) Rs 438.85 + Rs 256.75   (c) ₹ 1238.40 + ₹ 5379.60

   (d) Rs 27.25 + Rs 15.30 + Rs 196.00   (e) ₹ 4126.65 + ₹ 758.20 + ₹ 3336.30

Subtract.

5. (a)
Rs   p

| | 8 0 |
| − | 4 5 |

(b)
Rs   p

| | 7 0 |
| − | 2 5 |

(c)
Rs   p

| | 5 5 | 4 5 |
| − | 2 6 | 2 5 |

(d)
Rs   p

| | 9 7 | 2 5 |
| − | 6 8 | 5 0 |

(e)
Rs   p

| | 8 7 | 0 0 |
| − | 3 9 | 2 5 |

6. (a) Rs 763.25
   − Rs   28.45

(b) Rs 835.00
   − Rs 259.85

(c) ₹ 4218.75
   − ₹ 159.40

(d) ₹ 7500.25
   − ₹ 1249.45

7. (a) Rs 158.20 − Rs 32.90   (b) Rs 679.00 − Rs 128.65   (c) ₹ 2216.55 − ₹ 1038.95

8. (a) Rs 127 − Rs 15.70   (b) Rs 408 − Rs 327.25   (c) ₹ 5000 − ₹ 354.50

Multiplication of Money

Multiply money in the same way you multiply ordinary numbers. For longer sums, write the rupees and paise in separate columns or with a point between them.

30 p × 5 = ___150 p___

Rs 15 × 4 = ___Rs 60___

Rs 400 × 3 = ___Rs 1200___

Find 25 p × 7.

```
      p
    1 3
    2 5
  ×   7
  ─────
  1 7 5 p
```

175 p = Rs 1.75

25 p × 7 = 175 p
        = Re 1 + 75 p
Write 75 in paise's
position. Carry Re 1.

```
      1 3
  Re 0.25
  ×     7
  ───────
  Rs 1.75
```

Multiply ₹ 36.45 by 4.

```
   2 1  2
  ₹ 3 6.4 5
  ×       4
  ─────────
  ₹ 1 4 5.8 0
```

45 p × 4 = 180 p = ₹ 1 + 80 p
Write 80 in paise's position.
Carry ₹ 1 and multiply.

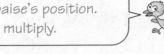

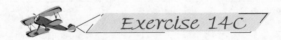

Exercise 14C

Multiply.

1. (a) 15 p × 5 =   (b) 50 p × 6 =   (c) 60 p × 3 =   (d) 300 p × 7 =

   (e) Rs 8 × 9 =   (f) Rs 12 × 4 =   (g) Rs 90 × 2 =   (h) Rs 200 × 5 =

2. (a)
```
  Rs 23.40
  ×      2
```

   (b)
```
  Rs 15.25
  ×      4
```

   (c)
```
  Re  0.45
  ×      6
```

   (d)
```
  Rs 72.50
  ×      8
```

   (e)
```
  Rs 87.65
  ×      6
```

   (f)
```
  Rs 90.75
  ×      7
```

   (g)
```
  Rs 101.00
  ×       4
```

   (h)
```
  Rs 165.95
  ×       6
```

3. (a) 95 p × 7   (b) Rs 48 × 6   (c) Re 0.75 × 5   (d) Rs 16.00 × 4

   (e) ₹ 38.35 × 9   (f) ₹ 83.50 × 7   (g) ₹ 450.65 × 3   (h) ₹ 907.25 × 5

Division of Money

Divide money in the same way you divide ordinary numbers.

$$65\,p \div 13 = 5\,p \qquad 700\,p \div 7 = 100\,p \qquad ₹\,72 \div 9 = ₹\,8$$

Divide 48 rupees and 32 paise by 8.

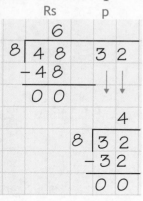

You may write the rupees and paise in separate columns and divide them separately, as shown.

Or, separate the rupees and paise with a point. Divide the rupees first. Put a point after the quotient of this division. Then divide the paise.

Q = Rs 6 and 4 p = Rs 6.04

Q = Rs 6.04

Exercise 14D

Divide.

1. (a) 45 p ÷ 9 =   (b) 500 p ÷ 5 =   (c) Rs 14 ÷ 2 =   (d) Rs 18 ÷ 3 =

   (e) Rs 32 ÷ 4 =   (f) Rs 36 ÷ 6 =   (g) Rs 63 ÷ 7 =   (h) Rs 900 ÷ 9 =

2. (a) Rs
       6 | 4 2 . 6 0

   (b) Rs
       4 | 2 8 . 2 0

   (c) Rs
       5 | 3 5 . 0 5

   (d) Rs
       7 | 5 6 . 7 0

3. (a) 8 rupees 80 paise ÷ 4   (b) 12 rupees 60 paise ÷ 6   (c) 30 rupees 50 paise ÷ 5

4. (a) Rs 24.00 ÷ 2   (b) Rs 81.00 ÷ 9   (c) Rs 25.05 ÷ 5   (d) Rs 48.15 ÷ 3

   (e) ₹ 42.35 ÷ 7   (f) ₹ 72.40 ÷ 8   (g) ₹ 54.30 ÷ 6   (h) ₹ 60.75 ÷ 5

Word Sums

1. Radha bought a pen for Rs 20, an eraser for Rs 7.50 and a card for Rs 15.50. Make a bill for her.

	Rs	p
Pen	20	00
Eraser	7	50
Card	15	50
Total	43	00

2. Farukh bought a bag for Rs 425 and a cap for Rs 225.50. He gave a 2000-rupee note to the shopkeeper. How much money did the shopkeeper return?

Rs 425.00
+ Rs 225.50
Rs 650.50

Rs 2000.00
− Rs 650.50
Rs 1349.50

The shopkeeper returned Rs 1349.50.

3. A dozen (12) bananas costs ₹ 22.50. How much does Madhu pay for 2 dozen bananas?

₹ 22.50
× 2
₹ 45.00

Madhu pays ₹ 45.

4. Murali had ₹ 40.50. He bought 3 small cups of vanilla ice cream with the money. How much did each cup cost?

```
      ₹
      13.50
  3 ) 40.50
    − 3
      10
     − 9
      15
     −15
      000
       − 0
         0
```

Each cup cost ₹ 13.50.

Exercise 14-E

1. Make a bill: Tea Rs 40.50, sugar Rs 39.50, milk Rs 22.

2. Asdar bought a T-shirt for Rs 375. He gave a 500-rupee note to the shopkeeper. How much money did the shopkeeper return?

3. Jatin bought 6 pastries for Rs 15 each. How much did he pay?

4. Mala got Rs 360 by selling 6 of her large flower pots. For how much did she sell each pot?

5. Do these sums in your notebook.

   (a) Make a bill: Chair Rs 1200, table Rs 2570, cupboard Rs 5895.

   (b) Soni got Rs 51 from her grandma, Rs 100.50 from her grandpa and Rs 250.50 from her cousin. How much money did she get in all?

   (c) Jaya's sari cost Rs 950. If Leena's sari cost Rs 125 less, how much did it cost?

   (d) Mr Sharma went to the market with Rs 250. He spent Rs 45 on milk, Rs 125 on sweets and Rs 75 on apples. How much money was he left with?

   (e) Hari earns ₹ 143.65 every day. How much does he earn in a week?

   (f) Nita's doll costs ₹ 243. Raghu's remote-controlled car costs 4 times as much as the doll. How much does Raghu's car cost?

   (g) A group of children paid ₹ 248 for tickets at the zoo. If 1 ticket was for ₹ 8, how many children were there in the group?

Review Worksheet 4

1. Match.

$\frac{1}{2}$

$\frac{1}{3}$

$\frac{2}{3}$

$\frac{1}{4}$

$\frac{3}{4}$

2. Colour to show the fractions.

$\frac{2}{3}$

$\frac{1}{3}$

$\frac{1}{4}$

$\frac{3}{4}$

$\frac{1}{2}$

3. Fill in.

(a) You can draw _____ straight line joining two points.

(b) In a square, _____ sides are equal.

(c) A cuboid has _____ faces and _____ edges.

(d) A cylinder has _____ flat faces, _____ curved face and _____ edges.

(e) 50 p = Re _____   (f) Rs 62.50 = _____ p   (g) 7300 p = Rs _____

(h) $\frac{1}{2}$ of 8 = _____   (i) $\frac{1}{3}$ of 15 = _____   (j) $\frac{1}{4}$ of 4 = _____

Do these sums in your notebook.

4. (a) Rs 35.60 + Rs 125.70   (b) Rs 27.55 + Rs 432.80 + Rs 4287

5. (a) Rs 79 – Rs 46.50   (b) Rs 3413.75 – Rs 596

6. (a) Rs 68.95 × 7   (b) Rs 542.85 × 6

7. (a) Rs 81.30 ÷ 3   (b) 65 rupees 50 paise ÷ 5

15. Time

We use hours, minutes and seconds to measure time.
A second is a very short period of time. You would take a second or two to run across your classroom. But you would take about 52 seconds to sing *Jana Gana Mana*. You can say that we take close to a minute to sing our national anthem. That is because 60 seconds make a minute. A minute is a longer period than a second. And an hour is longer than a minute. 60 minutes make an hour.

Telling the Time

Clocks and watches show the time of the day.
They usually have hour and minute hands.
Some watches also have a second hand. The
second hand moves quickly. It moves round
the dial of a watch in 60 seconds (1 minute).

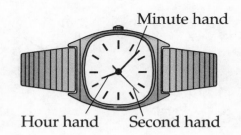

Minute hand
Hour hand   Second hand

See how the minute and hour hands move in an hour (60 minutes).

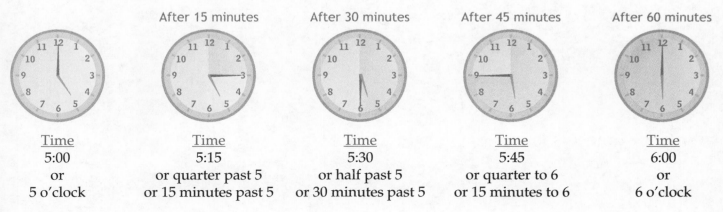

| After 15 minutes | After 30 minutes | After 45 minutes | After 60 minutes |

Time	Time	Time	Time	Time
5:00	5:15	5:30	5:45	6:00
or	or quarter past 5	or half past 5	or quarter to 6	or
5 o'clock	or 15 minutes past 5	or 30 minutes past 5	or 15 minutes to 6	6 o'clock

The minute hand goes from one number to the next in
5 minutes.
When it is at 12, the time shown is the hour of the day.
When at 1, it shows 1 × 5 = 5 minutes past the hour,
when at 2, it shows 2 × 5 = 10 minutes past the hour,
when at 3, it shows 3 × 5 = 15 minutes past the hour,
and so on. So, you can use the multiplication table of
5 to tell the number of minutes past the hour.

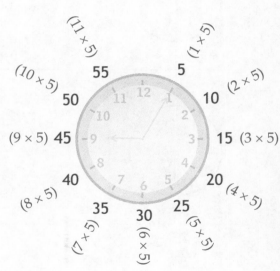

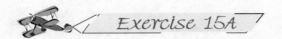

Exercise 15A

Write the time as shown.

7 o'clock

Write the time as shown.

  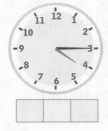  

3 : 05

Write the time as shown.

quarter past six   20 minutes past two

126

Draw the hands to show the time.

half past 9

20 minutes past six

quarter to three

fifty minutes past two

How much time has passed?

10 minutes

Other Measures of Time

To measure long periods of time we use days, weeks, months and years.

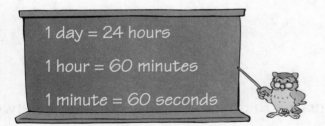

1 day = 24 hours

1 hour = 60 minutes

1 minute = 60 seconds

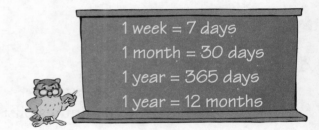

1 week = 7 days

1 month = 30 days

1 year = 365 days

1 year = 12 months

Change 4 hours 10 minutes to minutes.

1 hour = 60 minutes.

∴ 4 hours = 4 x 60 minutes = 240 minutes.

∴ 4 hours 10 minutes = 240 minutes + 10 minutes

= 250 minutes.

Change 2 minutes 25 seconds to seconds.

1 minute = 60 seconds.

∴ 2 minutes = 2 x 60 seconds = 120 seconds.

∴ 2 minutes 25 seconds

= 120 seconds + 25 seconds

= 145 seconds.

Change 3 days to hours.

1 day = 24 hours.

∴ 3 days = 3 x 24 hours = 72 hours.

Change 2 months 3 weeks to days.

1 month = 30 days.

∴ 2 months = 2 x 30 days = 60 days.

1 week = 7 days.

∴ 3 weeks = 3 x 7 days = 21 days.

∴ 2 months 3 weeks

= 60 days + 21 days = 81 days.

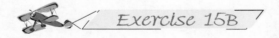

Exercise 15B

1. Fill in.

   (a) 4 hours = _____ minutes   (b) 2 days = _____ hours

   (c) 3 weeks = _____ days   (d) 4 months = _____ days

   (e) 7 minutes = _____ seconds   (f) 1 week = _____ hours

2. Change:

   (a) 6 hours to minutes   (b) 4 hours 12 minutes to minutes

   (c) 5 minutes to seconds   (d) 9 minutes 35 seconds to seconds

   (e) 8 days to hours   (f) 10 days 23 hours to hours

   (g) 5 weeks to days   (h) 7 weeks 4 days to days

   (i) 9 months to days   (j) 3 months 14 days to days

   (k) 2 days 4 hours to hours   (l) 8 hours 12 minutes to minutes

   (m) 2 weeks to hours   (n) 3 months 3 weeks to days

3. Write these dates in the order in which they come in the year.

15 August (Independence Day) _____

2 October (Gandhi Jayanti) _____

26 January (Republic Day) _____

5 September (Teachers' Day) _____

14 November (Children's Day) _____

4. Write in the order in which these were invented.

Computer mouse: 1963 _____

Light bulb: 1860 _____

Aeroplane: 1903 _____

Safety pin: 1849 _____

Television: 1926 _____

5. Write these dates in the order in which they came.

4 July 2005 _____

8 March 2010 _____

7 February 2009 _____

15 December 2003 _____

21 May 2009 _____

6. Sourav is 4 years older than Ishani. Ishani was born in 2009.
In which year was Sourav born?

7. The motorcycle was invented in 1885. The helicopter was
invented 22 years later. When was the helicopter invented?

8. Javed's school will be closed for 10 days starting from
24 December. When will his school reopen?

16. Measures of Length

To measure the length of a thing, we need to compare it with a fixed length.
The centimetre is a fixed length we use to measure small lengths such as the length of a book, the height of a TV set and the thickness of a mobile phone.
Centimetre is written as cm in short. The big marks on the ruler below are 1 cm apart.

You can use a ruler to measure line segments like AB.
Place the edge of the ruler along the line. The 0 mark should be at one end. The other end (point B) is at the 5-cm mark. So AB measures 5 cm or AB = 5 cm. Now measure the red and green line segments below.

C _____ D   CD = _____

P _____ Q   PQ = _____

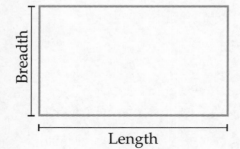

Measure the sides of this rectangle.
The measurement of a longer side is called length.
The measurement of a shorter side is called breadth.
Length = _____   Breadth = _____
Sum of the sides = length + breadth + length + breadth
= _____

Measure the sides of this triangle.
Side 1 = _____   Side 2 = _____   Side 3 = _____
Sum of the sides = Side 1 + Side 2 + Side 3
= _____

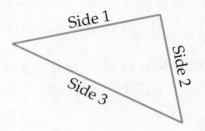

To measure bigger lengths, we use a bigger fixed length called the metre. Lengths of cloth, wire, etc., are usually measured in metres. 1 metre is 1 m in short.

| 1 m = 100 cm |

Lata's chunri is 2 m long.

That means it is 1 m + 1 m = 100 cm + 100 cm
= 2 × 100 cm = 200 cm long.

To change m into cm, multiply by 100 or put 2 zeros on the right.

A carpet is 3 m 10 cm long. Change the length into centimetres.

3 m 10 cm = 3 m + 10 cm
= 300 cm + 10 cm = 310 cm.

To change m and cm into cm, change the m to cm and then add the cm.

Susan's father's height is 176 cm. Change into m and cm.

1 m = 100 cm. To find how many metres, divide by 100.

176 ÷ 100 = 1 and remainder 76.

So, 176 cm = 1 m 76 cm.

Changing cm into m and cm
Divide the number of cm by 100.
Quotient is in m, remainder is in cm.
Use the short cut for dividing by 100.

The metre is not used to measure large lengths like the distance between your house and your school. We use the kilometre (km in short) to measure large distances.

Find out how far these places are from your home:

Your school _____ km   Police station _____ km

Railway station _____ km   Hospital _____ km

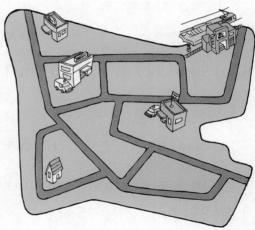

1 km = 1000 m

Mr Malik walked 3 km.

He walked 1 km + 1 km + 1 km
= 1000 m + 1000 m + 1000 m
= 3 × 1000 m = 3000 m.

To change km into m, multiply by 1000 or put 3 zeros on the right.

The market is 4 km 500 m from Sonu's house. Change the distance to metres.

4 km 500 m = 4 km + 500 m
= 4000 m + 500 m = 4500 m.

Changing km and m into m
Change km to m (multiply by 1000).
Add the metres.

Change 6452 m to km and m.

1 km = 1000 m. To find how many km, divide by 1000.

6452 ÷ 1000 = 6 and remainder 452.

So, 6452 m = 6 km 452 m.

Changing m to km and m
Divide the number of m by 1000.
Quotient is in km, remainder is in m.
Use the short cut for dividing by 1000.

131

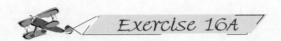

Change into centimetres.

1. (a) 3 m = _____   (b) 7 m = _____   (c) 17 m = _____   (d) 56 m = _____

2. (a) 5 m 90 cm   (b) 28 m 75 cm   (c) 35 m 18 cm   (d) 47 m 9 cm   (e) 99 m 7 cm

3. Change into metres.

   (a) 400 cm = ____   (b) 600 cm = ____   (c) 1000 cm = ____   (d) 3500 cm = ____

4. Change into metres and centimetres.

   (a) 318 cm   (b) 649 cm   (c) 508 cm   (d) 1342 cm   (e) 7584 cm   (f) 2006 cm

Change into metres.

5. (a) 4 km = _____   (b) 6 km = _____   (c) 82 km = _____   (d) 90 km = _____

6. (a) 3 km 143 m   (b) 6 km 375 m   (c) 4 km 72 m   (d) 9 km 5 m   (e) 6 km 7 m

Change into kilometres.

7. (a) 3000 m = _____   (b) 5000 m = _____   (c) 6000 m = _____   (d) 8000 m = _____

Change into kilometres and metres.

8. (a) 3512 m   (b) 2589 m   (c) 6342 m   (d) 5600 m   (e) 4080 m   (f) 7004 m

Adding and Subtracting Lengths

To add or subtract lengths, write the number of km, m and cm in separate columns. Then add or subtract like ordinary numbers, starting from the right-hand column.

Find 304 m 32 cm + 96 m 28 cm + 8 m 9 cm.

m	cm
3 0 4	3 2
+ 9 6	2 8
+ 8	9
4 0 8	6 9

Ans. 408 m 69 cm

Find 25 km 320 m − 17 km 16 m.

km	m
2̶5̶	3̶2̶0̶
− 1 7	1 6
0 8	3 0 4

Ans. 8 km 304 m

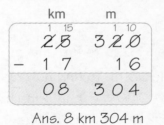

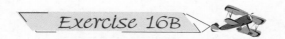
Add.

1. (a)
```
      cm
    3 9
  + 2 6
```
(b)
```
       m
    2 4 3
  + 5 8 9
```
(c)
```
      km
    3 8
  + 5 7
```
(d)
```
     m   cm
   2 5  6 2
 + 3 9  1 8
```
(e)
```
    km    m
   4   2 6 4
 + 2   1 5 8
```

2. (a) 45 cm + 25 cm   (b) 78 cm + 17 cm   (c) 20 cm + 36 cm + 7 cm   (d) 57 cm + 39 cm

   (e) 243 m + 589 m   (f) 283 m + 148 m   (g) 18 km + 45 km   (h) 379 km + 268 km

3. (a) 67 m 35 cm + 98 m 38 cm   (b) 256 m 49 cm + 428 m 50 cm

   (c) 67 m 20 cm + 25 m 28 cm + 7 m 2 cm   (d) 354 m 35 cm + 76 m 28 cm + 8 m 7 cm

4. (a) 42 km 369 m + 17 km 441 m   (b) 157 km 225 m + 385 km 675 m

   (c) 875 km 238 m + 19 km 29 m   (d) 732 km 574 m + 65 km 103 m + 67 m

Subtract.

5. (a)
```
      cm
    3 5
  - 1 7
```
(b)
```
       m
    5 7
  - 2 8
```
(c)
```
      km
    7 3
  - 2 5
```
(d)
```
     m   cm
   4 3  3 2
 - 1 7  1 5
```
(e)
```
    km    m
   6 5  8 3 2
 - 2 9  5 6 8
```

6. (a) 54 cm – 29 cm   (b) 46 cm – 38 cm   (c) 75 cm – 16 cm   (d) 94 cm – 47 cm

   (e) 368 m – 169 m   (f) 32 km – 18 km   (g) 65 km – 46 km   (h) 462 km – 85 km

7. (a) 25 m 72 cm – 9 m 56 cm   (b) 42 m 51 cm – 27 m 17 cm   (c) 93 m 12 cm – 36 m

8. (a) 48 km 655 m – 9 km 276 m   (b) 71 km 810 m – 32 km 548 m   (c) 24 km 548 m – 13 km

Multiplying Lengths

To multiply lengths, write the number of km, m and cm in separate columns. Then multiply in the same way you multiply ordinary numbers.

Find 23 m × 3.

```
      m
    2 3
  ×   3
  ─────
    6 9
```
Ans. 69 m

133

Find 16 m 17 cm × 3.

m	cm
¹1 6	²1 7
×	3
48	51	Ans. 48 m 51 cm

Multiply the cm first and then the m. Similarly, multiply the m first and then the km.

Find 43 km 153 m × 5.

km	m
¹4 3	²1 ¹5 3
×	5
215	765	Ans. 215 km 765 m

Exercise 16C

Multiply.

1. (a)

cm	
2 3	
× 4	

(b)

m	
1 9	
× 6	

(c)

km	
2 7	
× 8	

(d)

m	cm
1 6	2 1
×	4

(e)

km	m
7 6	1 5 4
×	3

2. (a) 18 cm × 3   (b) 37 cm × 2   (c) 21 cm × 4   (d) 49 m × 6   (e) 116 m × 8
    (f) 167 m × 5   (g) 17 km × 6   (h) 35 km × 7   (i) 185 km × 9   (j) 238 km × 3

3. (a) 37 m 49 cm × 2   (b) 28 m 14 cm × 7   (c) 43 m 17 cm × 5   (d) 52 m 13 cm × 6

4. (a) 64 km 121 m × 8   (b) 32 km 192 m × 4   (c) 58 km 423 m × 2   (d) 72 km 325 m × 3

Dividing Lengths

To divide lengths, write the number of km, m and cm in their own columns.
Then divide them separately like ordinary numbers.

Divide 245 m 95 cm by 5.

```
        m      cm
        4 9
    5 2 4 5    9 5
      - 2 0
        4 5
      - 4 5
        0 0
                1 9
            5 9 5
              - 5
              4 5
            - 4 5
              0 0
```

Ans. 49 m 19 cm.

Divide the m before dividing the cm. Similarly, divide the km before dividing the m.

Divide 84 km 742 m by 7.

```
        km       m
        1 2
    7 8 4     7 4 2
      - 7
      1 4
    - 1 4
      0 0     1 0 6
          7 7 4 2
            - 7
            0 4
            - 0
            4 2
          - 4 2
            0 0
```

Ans. 12 km 106 m.

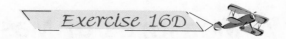

Find.

1. (a) 96 cm ÷ 6   (b) 81 cm ÷ 9   (c) 68 cm ÷ 4   (d) 76 m ÷ 4   (e) 465 m ÷ 5

   (f) 602 m ÷ 7   (g) 177 m ÷ 3   (h) 300 km ÷ 4   (i) 522 km ÷ 6   (j) 776 km ÷ 8

2. (a) 28 m 56 cm ÷ 2   (b) 396 m 45 cm ÷ 3   (c) 605 m 90 cm ÷ 5   (d) 328 m 64 cm ÷ 8

3. (a) 52 km 16 m ÷ 4   (b) 72 km 426 m ÷ 6   (c) 147 km 105 m ÷ 7   (d) 906 km 480 m ÷ 3

Do and Learn

Aim To make a measuring tape and measure around things

Things needed A ribbon (or a string), ballpoint pen, a 30-cm ruler, things with a curved face

Do and Learn

1. Tape the ribbon to the ruler and make centimetre marks with a ballpoint pen. Now you have a measuring tape like the ones tailors have. Use it to measure lengths along curved faces.

   Write to the nearest cm. For example, if something is a little more or a little less than 5 cm, write 5 cm.

Your wrist	
Your ankle	
Your neck	
A pen	
A cup	
A glass	

17. Measures of Mass

How much something weighs depends on its mass. The more mass something has, the more is its weight. So, we often use the word 'weight' for 'mass'.
To weigh something, we compare its mass with that of fixed weights using a balance.
Fixed weights used to weigh light things are in grams (g in short).
Those used to weigh heavy things are in kilograms (kg in short).

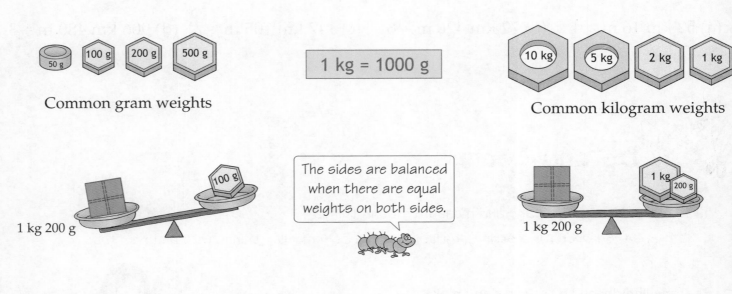

Common gram weights

1 kg = 1000 g

Common kilogram weights

The sides are balanced when there are equal weights on both sides.

1 kg 200 g

1 kg 200 g

Write correct weights to balance the sides.

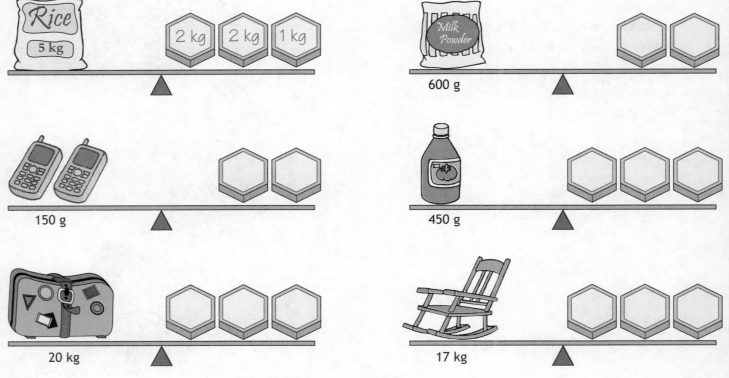

Change 2 kg into grams.

2 kg = 1 kg + 1 kg = 1000 g + 1000 g
= 2 × 1000 g = 2000 g.

To change kg into g, multiply by 1000 or put 3 zeros on the right.

Change 3 kg 260 g into grams.

3 kg 260 g = 3 kg + 260 g
= 3000 g + 260 g = 3260 g.

To change kg and g to g, change the kg to g and then add the g.

Change 8000 g into kg.

1 kg = 1000 g.
To find how many kg, divide by 1000.
8000 ÷ 1000 = 8.
So, 8000 g = 8 kg.

Change 6054 g into kg and g.

6054 ÷ 1000 = 6 and remainder 54.
So, 6054 g = 6 kg 54 g.

Changing g into kg and g
Divide the number of g by 1000.
Quotient is in kg, remainder is in g.

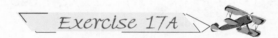
Exercise 17A

Change into grams.

1. (a) 3 kg = _____ (b) 7 kg = _____ (c) 8 kg = _____ (d) 9 kg = _____

2. (a) 5 kg 700 g (b) 3 kg 60 g (c) 2 kg 97 g (d) 4 kg 9 g (e) 3 kg 608 g (f) 1 kg 5 g

3. Change into kilograms.

(a) 4000 g = _____ (b) 2000 g = _____ (c) 7000 g = _____ (d) 9000 g = _____

4. Change into kilograms and grams.
(a) 7629 g (b) 6903 g (c) 8200 g (d) 7004 g (e) 1357 g (f) 3048 g

Adding and Subtracting Masses

To add or subtract masses, write the number of kg and g in separate columns. Then add or subtract like ordinary numbers, starting from the right-hand column.

Find 42 kg 564 g + 673 kg 76 g + 259 g.

```
        kg        g
    ¹           ¹  ¹
        4 2    5 6 4
  +  6 7 3       7 6
  +              2 5 9
     7 1 5    8 9 9
```
Ans. 715 kg 899 g

Find 7629 kg 847 g – 3848 kg 79 g.

```
        kg          g
   6  15            7  13
      ₇ 12             ₇ 17
    7 6 2 9      8 4 7
  – 3 8 4 8        7 9
    3 7 8 1      7 6 8
```
Ans. 3781 kg 768 g

137

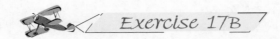

Add.

1. (a)
	g
	4 2 8
+	3 9 7

(b)
	g
	2 7 4
+	3 5 6

(c)
	kg	g
	2 4	3 6 7
+	6 3	4 8 6

(d)
	kg	g
	1 5 6	5 7 4
+	4 6 8	2 5 6

2. (a) 468 g + 219 g   (b) 128 g + 352 g + 257 g   (c) 276 g + 159 g + 98 g + 208 g

3. (a) 8972 kg + 258 kg   (b) 57 kg + 49 kg + 375 kg   (c) 4127 kg + 376 kg + 538 kg

4. (a) 35 kg 492 g + 67 kg 308 g   (b) 460 kg 540 g + 356 kg 37 g + 28 kg 200 g
   (c) 26 kg 349 g + 157 kg 50 g + 37 kg 8 g   (d) 120 kg 260 g + 315 kg 210 g + 7 g
   (e) 1857 kg 164 g + 367 kg + 17 kg 79 g   (f) 2321 kg + 6452 kg 125 g + 7 kg 690 g

Subtract.

5. (a)
	g
	6 4 3
−	5 2 8

(b)
	kg
	2 7 1
−	8 5

(c)
	kg	g
	1 8	5 6 3
−	1 1	3 6 4

(d)
	kg	g
	8 4 9	6 7 8
−	5 6 9	2 8 7

6. (a) 812 g − 471 g   (b) 714 g − 168 g   (c) 976 g − 389 g   (d) 606 g − 315 g

7. (a) 632 kg − 98 kg   (b) 742 kg − 367 kg   (c) 3465 kg − 769 kg   (d) 2943 kg − 1687 kg

8. (a) 8 kg 734 g − 2 kg 26 g   (b) 75 kg 846 g − 46 kg 658 g   (c) 90 kg 473 g − 61 kg 168 g
   (d) 450 kg 642 g − 187 g   (e) 502 kg 630 g − 146 kg 75 g   (f) 6348 kg 925 g − 2657 kg

Multiplying Masses

Find 2145 kg 247 g × 4.

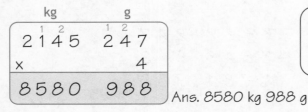

Ans. 8580 kg 988 g

Multiply masses the way you multiply ordinary numbers. Write the kg and g in separate columns. Multiply the g first and then the kg.

Multiply.

1. (a)

g	
1 4 2	
×	3

(b)

kg	
4 7 5	
×	5

(c)

kg	g
3	2 7 6
×	3

(d)

kg	g
6 4	1 4 8
×	4

2. (a) 24 g × 6   (b) 125 g × 7   (c) 120 g × 8   (d) 109 g × 9

3. (a) 87 kg × 3   (b) 352 kg × 5   (c) 568 kg × 6   (d) 1639 kg × 4

4. (a) 23 kg 255 g × 3   (b) 84 kg 175 g × 5   (c) 55 kg 218 g × 4

   (d) 105 kg 456 g × 2   (e) 550 kg 164 g × 6   (f) 3245 kg 296 g × 3

Dividing Masses

Divide 54 kg 126 g by 6.

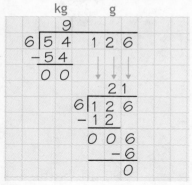

Divide masses the way you divide ordinary numbers. Write the kg and g in separate columns. Divide the kg first and then the g.

Ans. 9 kg 21 g.

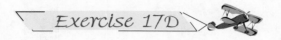

Find.

1. (a) 96 g ÷ 4   (b) 305 g ÷ 5   (c) 856 g ÷ 8   (d) 891 g ÷ 9

2. (a) 72 kg ÷ 6   (b) 816 kg ÷ 3   (c) 408 kg ÷ 4   (d) 6216 kg ÷ 6

3. (a) 36 kg 93 g ÷ 3   (b) 64 kg 24 g ÷ 4   (c) 40 kg 608 g ÷ 2   (d) 525 kg 450 g ÷ 5

   (e) 798 kg 917 g ÷ 7   (f) 120 kg 630 g ÷ 6   (g) 872 kg 400 g ÷ 8   (h) 648 kg 594 g ÷ 9

18. Measures of Capacity

Liquids are measured in millilitres (mL in short) and litres (L in short). Small amounts of liquids, like medicines, are measured in millilitres. Large amounts of liquids, like petrol, are measured in litres.

$$1 \text{ L} = 1000 \text{ mL}$$

The amount of liquid something can hold is called its capacity. For example, the capacity of a teaspoon is 5 mL. Buckets and bottles of different sizes hold different amounts of liquids.

5 mL   500 mL   10 L

Match.

5 medicine caps with 10 mL of liquid in each   100-mL cup half full   100-mL cup full

Five 100-mL cups   300-mL bottle   500-mL bottle

Two 500-mL bottles   1-L flask full   1-L flask half full

Ten 500-mL mugs   10-L bucket full   10-L bucket half full

Change 2 L into millilitres.

2 L = 1 L + 1 L = 1000 mL + 1000 mL
   = 2 × 1000 mL = 2000 mL.

To change L into mL, multiply by 1000 or put 3 zeros on the right.

Change 7 L 30 mL into mL.

7 L 30 mL = 7 L + 30 mL
          = 7000 mL + 30 mL = 7030 mL.

To change L and mL to mL, change the L to mL and then add the mL.

Change 5000 mL into litres.

1 L = 1000 mL.
To find how many L, divide by 1000.
5000 ÷ 1000 = 5.
So, 5000 mL = 5 L.

Change 7032 mL into L and mL.

7032 ÷ 1000 = 7 and remainder 32.
So, 7032 mL = 7 L 32 mL.

Changing mL into L and mL
Divide the number of mL by 1000.
Quotient is in L, remainder is in mL.

Exercise 18A

Change into millilitres.

1. (a) 3 L = _____   (b) 7 L = _____   (c) 6 L = _____   (d) 8 L = _____

2. (a) 7 L 400 mL   (b) 3 L 98 mL   (c) 2 L 45 mL   (d) 9 L 302 mL   (e) 5 L 5 mL

3. Change into litres.

   (a) 2000 mL = _____   (b) 3000 mL = _____   (c) 5000 mL = _____   (d) 7000 mL = _____

4. Change into litres and millilitres.

   (a) 1745 mL   (b) 4512 mL   (c) 2500 mL   (d) 4070 mL   (e) 8102 mL   (f) 3005 mL

Adding and Subtracting Liquid Measurements

To add or subtract liquid measurements, write the number of L and mL in separate columns. Then add or subtract like ordinary numbers, taking the millilitres first.

Find 32 L 346 mL + 17 L + 505 L 275 mL.

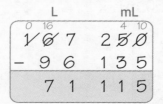

L	mL
3 2	3 4 6
+ 1 7	
+5 0 5	2 7 5
5 5 4	6 2 1

Ans. 554 L 621 mL

Find 167 L 250 mL – 96 L 135 mL.

L	mL
1 6 7	2 5 0
– 9 6	1 3 5
7 1	1 1 5

Ans. 71 L 115 mL

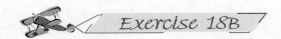

Add.

1. (a)
```
        mL
    3 5 2
  + 4 5 8
  ─────────
```

(b)
```
        L
    4 7 5
  + 3 4 8
  ─────────
```

(c)
```
    L      mL
  2 3    5 7 4
  + 5 8    2 4 6
  ───────────────
```

(d)
```
    L      mL
  1 5 6    2 2 4
  + 4 6 8    3 5 7
  ─────────────────
```

2. (a) 472 mL + 189 mL   (b) 260 mL + 575 mL   (c) 150 mL + 65 mL + 285 mL

3. (a) 407 L + 568 L   (b) 45 L + 165 L
   (c) 58 L + 345 L + 260 L   (d) 38 L + 65 L + 215 L + 340 L

4. (a) 6 L 155 mL + 9 L 368 mL   (b) 90 L 250 mL + 152 L 640 mL
   (c) 42 L 346 mL + 28 L 215 mL + 17 L 265 mL   (d) 123 L 456 mL + 746 L 214 mL
   (e) 345 L 40 mL + 38 L 125 mL + 257 L   (f) 3415 L 29 mL + 435 L + 907 mL

Subtract.

5. (a)
```
        mL
    7 6 8
  − 2 8 9
  ─────────
```

(b)
```
        L
    4 1 0
  − 1 7 5
  ─────────
```

(c)
```
    L      mL
  2 6    4 0 0
  −  7    1 7 2
  ───────────────
```

(d)
```
    L      mL
  7 8    5 1 0
  − 4 9      7 5
  ───────────────
```

6. (a) 250 mL – 67 mL   (b) 700 mL – 265 mL   (c) 930 mL – 463 mL   (d) 868 mL – 475 mL

7. (a) 72 L – 18 L   (b) 500 L – 243 L   (c) 125 L – 95 L   (d) 3729 L – 1968 L

8. (a) 6 L 345 mL – 3 L   (b) 65 L 250 mL – 52 L 163 mL
   (c) 250 L 625 mL – 138 L 57 mL   (d) 156 L 985 mL – 143 L 879 mL
   (e) 2100 L 210 mL – 1465 L 198 mL   (f) 3987 L 760 mL – 551 mL

Multiplying Liquid Measurements

Find 125 L 250 mL × 3.

```
    L      mL
   ¹      ¹
  1 2 5    2 5 0
  ×            3
  ───────────────
  3 7 5    7 5 0
```
Ans. 375 L 750 mL

> Multiply liquid measurements the way you multiply ordinary numbers. Write the L and mL in separate columns. Multiply the mL first and then the L.

Multiply.

1. (a)
	mL
	2 1 7
×	4

(b)
	L
	1 8 4
×	4

(c)
	L	mL
	2 5	2 9 5
×		3

(d)
	L	mL
	1 3 5	1 5 5
×		5

2. (a) 75 mL × 10   (b) 110 mL × 9   (c) 265 mL × 3   (d) 378 mL × 2

3. (a) 43 L × 7   (b) 536 L × 6   (c) 215 L × 5   (d) 1032 L × 4

4. (a) 7 L 158 mL × 6   (b) 36 L 178 mL × 4   (c) 125 L 105 mL × 8   (d) 357 L 140 mL × 5

Dividing Liquid Measurements

Divide 42 L 714 mL by 7.

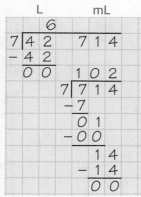

Ans. 6 L 102 mL

Divide the way you divide ordinary numbers.
Write the L and mL in separate columns.
Divide the L first and then the mL.

Find.

1. (a) 65 mL ÷ 5   (b) 392 mL ÷ 4   (c) 927 mL ÷ 9   (d) 816 mL ÷ 8

2. (a) 84 L ÷ 2   (b) 135 L ÷ 3   (c) 504 L ÷ 7   (d) 645 L ÷ 5

3. (a) 6 L 54 mL ÷ 6   (b) 75 L 350 mL ÷ 5   (c) 68 L 816 mL ÷ 4   (d) 171 L 855 mL ÷ 9

   (e) 288 L 448 mL ÷ 8   (f) 618 L 324 ml ÷ 6   (g) 805 L 490 mL ÷ 7   (h) 207 L 924 mL ÷ 3

19. Word Sums on Measurements

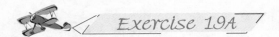

1. What length of pipe would you get by joining a pipe 4 m 20 cm long to another pipe 12 m 45 cm long?

2.  A piece of cloth measured 4 m 75 cm. A tailor used 2 m 60 cm from it . How much cloth was left?

3. A school bus made 3 trips to the zoo. It covered 17 km 320 m on each trip. What distance did it cover in total?

4.  Prabha used 12 m 90 cm of cloth to make 6 curtains of equal size. What length of cloth did she use to make each?

5. Mr Jain drove 17 km to reach his office. Then he drove to a shopping mall 5 km 750 m away. Later he drove another 12 km to his house. How far did he drive in all?

6. Shanta travelled 357 km by bus from Pune and then walked the rest of the way to her village. If the village is 365 km from Pune, how much did she walk?

7. Ijaz stuck 5 matchboxes to make a toy train. Each matchbox was 6 cm long. How long was the train?

8. A driver divided a 360-km journey into 3 equal parts. How many kilometres did he cover in each part?

1. Dola bought 750 g of potatoes and 500 g of peas. What was the total weight of the vegetables?

2. Lal bought 50 kg of cabbages and sold 37 kg. How much was left?

3. 400 g of sugar is used to bake 1 cake. How much sugar is needed to bake 3 cakes?

4. 4 children shared 500 g of peanuts equally. How much did each get?

5. Joe bought 5 kg wheat flour, 4 kg rice, 2 kg 500 g sugar and 250 g salt. What was the total weight of the groceries?

6. Rahul's weight is 27 kg less than his mother's weight. If his mother weighs 51 kg, what is his weight?

7. A carton of books weighs 36 kg 120 g. How much will 8 such cartons weigh?

8. A carpenter uses an equal amount of glue every day. If he uses 21 kg 350 g of glue in a week, how much glue does he use every day?

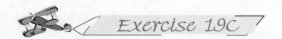

1. Harpreet bought 1 L of mustard oil, 1 L 500 mL of sunflower oil and 250 mL of olive oil. How much oil did she buy?

2. A milk booth had 400 L 600 mL of milk in the morning. By the evening it had 79 litres left. How much milk did it sell?

3. A painter bought four 5-L cans of paint. How much paint did he buy?

4. Madhavan divided 600 mL of juice equally among 4 glasses. How much juice did he pour into each glass?

5. A hospital uses 18 L 100 mL of liquid cleaner every month. How much cleaner does it use in 6 months?

6. Sonia's grandmother finished a 150-mL bottle of cough syrup in 10 days. She had the same amount of syrup every day. How much syrup did she have daily?

7. A family uses the same amount of water for washing every day. It needs 84 L 175 mL of water for washing in a week. How much water does it use daily?

8. A taxi driver uses 30 litres of petrol every day. How much petrol does he use in 7 days?

20. Data and Charts

Dhruv was making a list for a picnic.

He wrote: *Ankit, Priya and Anu like chicken roll; Pallavi, Bala, Vicky and Dev like samosa, ...*

His sister Mala told him that it would be better to make a table.

The table would make it easier to know how many of each thing to order.

So Dhruv called out the names and what they like, and Mala made / marks .

Then she added up the marks for ordering.

Food	How many like it	Number to order
Chicken roll	///	3
Samosa	////	4
Pastry	/////	5
Muffin	//	2

///// shows 5.

This table is a collection of facts and numbers.

It tells us things (facts) such as how many of Dhruv's friends like samosas.

We say that the table has data on what Dhruv's friends like to eat.

Dhruv thought of another way of showing this data.

He made a chart with pictures. A picture chart is called a pictograph.

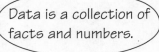

Data is a collection of facts and numbers.

147

Look at the pictograph below.

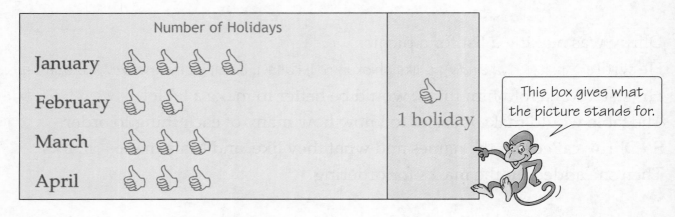

From this pictograph we know these things:

    1. The month with the most holidays is January (4).

    2. The months with the same number (3) of holidays are March and April.

    3. The month with the least holidays is February (2).

    4. The total number of holidays in the four months is 12.

Look at this pictograph and answer the questions.

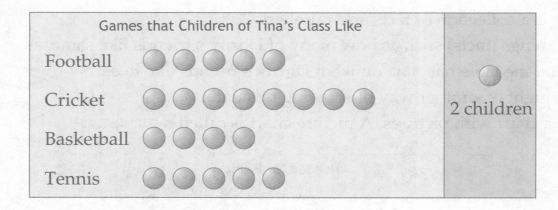

1. How many children like football? $5 \times 2 = 10$

2. How many children like tennis? _____

3. Which game is liked the most? _____ How many like it ? _____

4. Which game is liked the least? _____ How many like it ? _____

5. Which two games are liked equally? _____

Sometimes we have to use a part (a fraction) of a picture to show a number.

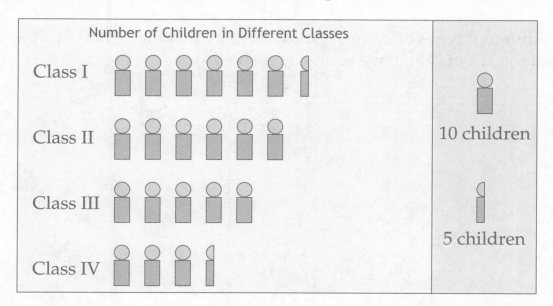

From the pictograph we can find the number of children in each class.

Class I: 6 × 10 + 5 = 65   Class II: 6 × 10 = 60

Class III: 5 × 10 = 50   Class IV: 3 × 10 + 5 = 35

We can make other kinds of charts to show what is given in the pictograph above. For example, we can make charts on squared paper. Two charts are shown here. In these, each coloured square shows 10 children.

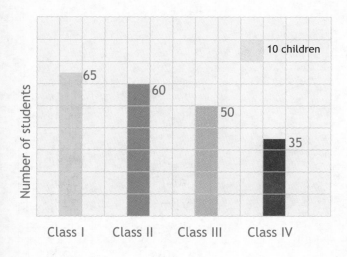

The coloured squares together look like bars. We call such charts bar charts or bar graphs.

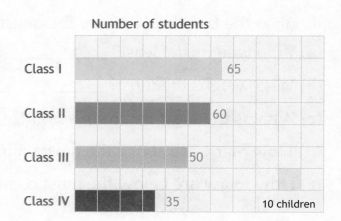

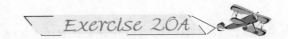
1. Gina has different types of sweets. Count them by making / marks in the table.
   (Cross out the sweets you have counted, as shown)

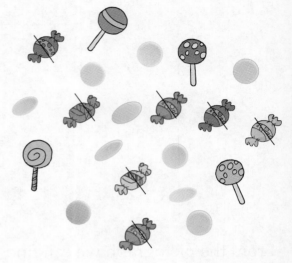

Sweet		Total
🍬	⁄⁄⁄⁄ ⁄⁄	7
🍭		

2. Ronny counted the pebbles, sticks and shells he had picked up at the beach. He took
   them out of a packet one by one and made / marks against their names. Write the
   total of each thing in the table.

Thing		Total
Stick	////	
Shell	⁄⁄⁄⁄ ⁄⁄⁄⁄ ///	
Pebble	⁄⁄⁄⁄ //	

3. Look at the table and answer the questions.

   (a) Who weighs the least? _____

   (b) Who weighs the most? _____

   (c) What is the most common weight? _____

   (d) How many are above the most common weight? _____

   (e) How many are below the most common weight? _____

Name	Weight
Jai	26 kg
Vijay	24 kg
Shyamal	25 kg
Ganesh	25 kg
Piyush	23 kg
Harsh	27 kg
Nitin	25 kg
Bobby	25 kg

4. If 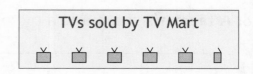 = 20 TVs and = 10 TVs, the total number of TVs sold in six days is _____.

TVs sold by TV Mart

5. If ◯ = 40 rotis then ◗ = 30 rotis, ◠ = 20 rotis and ◿ = 10 rotis. The total number of rotis made by Mrs Sharma in a week = _____.

6. This pictograph shows the number of children who took part in different things on Annual Day. Look at it and fill in the blanks.

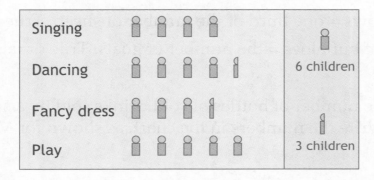

(a) The number of children who took part in the play = ___ and in the fancy dress = ___.
(b) The total number of children who took part = _____ .
(c) The least number took part in _____.

7. This pictograph shows how the children of a boarding school went home for their summer vacation.

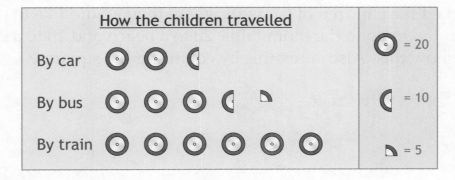

(a) The number of children who travelled by car = _____ .
(b) The number of children who travelled by bus = _____ .
(c) The number of children who travelled by train = _____ .

8. A farmer's son made a pictograph about the animals they own.

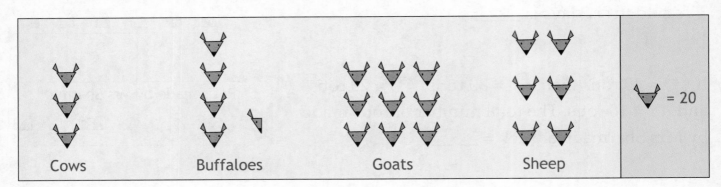

(a) The number of buffaloes + the number of sheep = _____ .

(b) They have _____ more buffaloes than cows.

(c) The number of cows = one third of the number of sheep. True or false? _____

(d) 2 × the number of buffaloes = the number of goats. True or false? _____

9. This chart shows the number of bottles of cold drinks sold by a shop in different months of a year. Write the numbers in the chart, as shown for March.

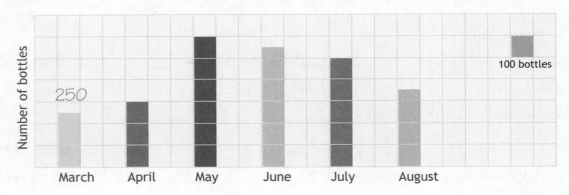

10. The teacher asked the children of Class III where they would like to go for a holiday. 20 children wanted to go to the mountains, 20 to a beach and 10 to a desert. Fill the pictograph to show this. Also show this by colouring the squares.

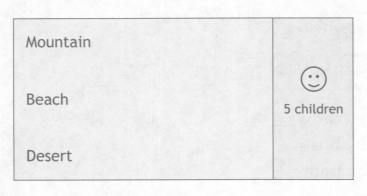

Review Worksheet 5

1. Write the time.

2. Fill in.

(a) 3 hours = _____ minutes   (b) 5 days = _____ hours

(c) 4 weeks = _____ days   (d) 3 months = _____ days

(e) 9 minutes = _____ seconds   (f) 2 weeks = _____ hours

(g) 7 metres = _____ cm   (h) 800 cm = _____ m

(i) 4000 m = _____ km   (j) 6 km = _____ m

(k) 5 kg = _____ grams   (l) 6000 grams = _____ kg

(m) 9000 mL = _____ L   (n) 2 L = _____ mL

3. Change:

   (a) 3 hours 5 minutes to minutes   (b) 7 days 13 hours to hours
   (c) 5 months 12 days to days   (d) 3 weeks 5 days to days
   (e) 2 L 32 mL to mL   (f) 1357 mL to litres and millilitres
   (g) 8 kg 300 g to grams   (h) 7168 grams to kilograms and grams
   (i) 9 m 20 cm to centimetres   (j) 601 cm to metres and centimetres

4. 25 children of a class come to school by bus and 15 children come by scooter. Colour the squares to show this.

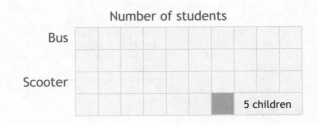

5. Find: (a) 46 km 387 m + 94 km 65 m   (b) 8 kg 608 g – 79 g   (c) 58 L 192 mL × 4

6. A box weighs 72 kg 120 g. How much will 7 such boxes weigh?

7. The children of a class got equal amounts of glue for each crafts class. If they used 486 mL of glue in 6 classes, how much glue did they get in each class?

153

Answers to Selected Exercises

Exercise 3A
1. (a) 1, 5, 10, 50, 100, 500, 1000   (b) 2, 3, 20, 30, 200, 300
   (c) 4, 9, 14, 19, 24, 29   (d) 6, 7, 8, 11, 12, 13, 16, 21, 25
2. (a) III, IV, I, II, IX, X, XI, XV, XIII, XVI
   (b) VII, V, VIII, XIV, XVIII, XIX, XII, VI, XVII, XX
3. See page 23   4. 2:00   8:00   3:30   10:30   4:30

Review Worksheet 1
1. Smallest number   368   304   579
   Greatest number   863   430   975
2. (a) 4000 + 600 + 70 + 2   (b) 6000 + 800 + 30 + 1
   (c) 5000 + 0 + 10 + 5   (d) 9000 + 700 + 0 + 8
3. (a) 1055, 1056, 1057, 1058, 1059, 1060
   (b) 3647, 3648, 3649, 3650, 3651, 3652
   (c) 8996, 8997, 8998, 8999, 9000, 9001
4. (a) > (b) > (c) < (d) <
5. (a) 6978, 6879, 5678, 5231, 3251
   (b) 9801, 9108, 8911, 8191, 8091
   (c) 7632, 7362, 6732, 6723, 6237
6. (a) 8, 10, 3000 respectively   (b) 4000, 50, 800 respectively
   (c) 11, 9, 6 respectively   (d) IV, VII, XIII respectively

Exercise 5A
1. (a) 75   (b) 91   (c) 65   (d) 361   (e) 165
   (f) 256   (g) 810   (h) 963   (i) 993   (j) 982
2. (a) 7867   (b) 2780   (c) 3777   (d) 6743   (e) 6471
   (f) 7342   (g) 6894   (h) 8785
3. (a) 91   (b) 46   (c) 75   (d) 82   (e) 92
4. (a) 372   (b) 665   (c) 895   (d) 880   (e) 982
5. (a) 6680   (b) 7874   (c) 8968   (d) 7882   (e) 8880
   (f) 8882   (g) 8977   (h) 6895
6. (a) 81   (b) 93   (c) 83   (d) 90   (e) 74
7. (a) 771   (b) 884   (c) 786   (d) 690   (e) 782
8. (a) 4685   (b) 9976   (c) 8783   (d) 9762

Exercise 5B
1. (a) 127   (b) 107   (c) 129   (d) 141   (e) 402
   (f) 544   (g) 847   (h) 512   (i) 824   (j) 800
2. (a) 6418   (b) 4800   (c) 7734   (d) 8635   (e) 8913
   (f) 3460   (g) 7631   (h) 9696
3. (a) 129   (b) 156   (c) 206   (d) 122   (e) 291
   (f) 641   (g) 476   (h) 985   (i) 821   (j) 900
4. (a) 3539   (b) 3971   (c) 8916   (d) 9789   (e) 7825
   (f) 7580   (g) 8820   (h) 9624
5. (a) 117   (b) 188   (c) 112   (d) 144   (e) 141
6. (a) 306   (b) 838   (c) 804   (d) 926   (e) 826
7. (a) 1727   (b) 5837   (c) 6860   (d) 7841

Exercise 5C
1. (a) 1196   (b) 1043   (c) 1057   (d) 1223   (e) 1616
2. (a) 2177   (b) 3049   (c) 4101   (d) 5341   (e) 4199
   (f) 6419   (g) 8000   (h) 8122
3. (a) 1579   (b) 1492   (c) 1455   (d) 2040   (e) 2501
4. (a) 8249   (b) 7562   (c) 9258   (d) 8200
5. (a) 1499   (b) 1374   (c) 1552   (d) 2281   (e) 2227
6. (a) 9058   (b) 8452   (c) 9133   (d) 8301
7. (a) 85   (b) 72   (c) 111   (d) 133   (e) 134
   (f) 452   (g) 900   (h) 841   (i) 1493   (j) 1030
   (k) 1302   (l) 1903   (m) 5831   (n) 5144   (o) 3330
   (p) 3822   (q) 5115   (r) 9022   (s) 5232   (t) 9000
   (u) 73   (v) 674   (w) 657   (x) 6031

Exercise 5D
1. 264   2. 574   3. 7030   4. 345
5. (a) 63 years   (b) 9476   (c) 7054   (d) 5014

Exercise 6A
1. (a) 18   (b) 39   (c) 18   (d) 14   (e) 13
   (f) 25   (g) 18   (h) 17   (i) 19   (j) 9
2. (a) 107   (b) 419   (c) 108   (d) 229   (e) 47
   (f) 248   (g) 226   (h) 53   (i) 574   (j) 534
3. (a) 2237   (b) 1303   (c) 3116   (d) 5029   (e) 16
   (f) 3957   (g) 28   (h) 1018

Exercise 6B
1. (a) 491   (b) 90   (c) 384   (d) 242   (e) 166
   (f) 586   (g) 371   (h) 58   (i) 654   (j) 75
2. (a) 4292   (b) 2399   (c) 2290   (d) 3128   (e) 7299

(f) 5557   (g) 2066   (h) 58
3. (a) 172   (b) 471   (c) 596   (d) 648   (e) 64
   (f) 105   (g) 279   (h) 47   (i) 2476   (j) 1088
   (k) 1065   (l) 84

Exercise 6C
1. (a) 4722   (b) 3661   (c) 1917   (d) 3790   (e) 894
   (f) 1866   (g) 1488   (h) 3148   (i) 3747   (j) 1909
   (k) 1435   (l) 1755
2. (a) 931   (b) 1868   (c) 1476   (d) 2577   (e) 467

Exercise 6D
1. (a) 84   (b) 78   (c) 10   (d) 28   (e) 16
2. (a) 218   (b) 286   (c) 148   (d) 162   (e) 227
   (f) 309   (g) 297   (h) 256   (i) 350   (j) 494
3. (a) 2209   (b) 4367   (c) 5989   (d) 6507   (e) 79
   (f) 889   (g) 1779   (h) 3489
4. (a) 39   (b) 97   (c) 656   (d) 737   (e) 217
   (f) 124   (g) 198   (h) 450   (i) 2689   (j) 988
   (k) 1898   (l) 2738

Exercise 6E
1. (a) 61   (b) 54   (c) 35   (d) 60   (e) 1   (f) 24   (g) 48   (h) 0
2. (a) 195   (b) 740   (c) 377   (d) 292   (e) 275   (f) 614   (g) 450   (h) 390
3. (a) 4927   (b) 0   (c) 1357   (d) 2418   (e) 1430   (f) 7637

Exercise 6F
1. 17   2. 33 years   3. 736   4. 3805
5. (a) 496   (b) 1214   (c) 6067   (d) 250   (e) 2672

Exercise 6G
3. 338   4. 1095   5. (a) 53   (b) Sunday   (c) 1527   (d) 2184

Review Worksheet 2
1. (a) 9000 + 700 + 80 + 3   (b) 543   (c) 709
   (d) Eight thousand seven hundred and five
   (e) 4040   (f) 7000, 100, 50 respectively
   (g) 50, 100, 7 respectively   (h) 4, 7, 20 respectively
   (i) VI, VIII, XIV respectively
2. (a) 7543   (b) 8113   (c) 5389   (d) 2527
3. (a) 894   (b) 180   (c) 1079   (d) 7028
4. (a) 882   (b) 237   (c) 7421   5. (a) 8915   (b) 876   (c) 564

Exercise 7B
1. (a) 48   (b) 39   (c) 28   (d) 66   (e) 84
   (f) 60   (g) 66   (h) 68   (i) 99   (j) 84
2. (a) 60   (b) 84   (c) 45   (d) 91   (e) 76
   (f) 81   (g) 50   (h) 78   (i) 70   (j) 92
3. (a) 128   (b) 116   (c) 105   (d) 184   (e) 265
   (f) 372   (g) 238   (h) 150   (i) 344   (j) 774
4. (a) 56   (b) 90   (c) 112   (d) 90   (e) 92
   (f) 204   (g) 270   (h) 171   (i) 392   (j) 576
   (k) 539   (l) 736

Exercise 7C
1. 64   2. 18   3. 36   4. 96
5. (a) 99   (b) 80   (c) 168
   (d) 270   (e) February (28 days)

Exercise 7D
1. (a) 224   (b) 426   (c) 808   (d) 963   (e) 900
2. (a) 436   (b) 690   (c) 402   (d) 795   (e) 1228
   (f) 872   (g) 975   (h) 928   (i) 927   (j) 756
3. (a) 1008   (b) 1068   (c) 1020   (d) 1035   (e) 1872
   (f) 2990   (g) 5787   (h) 1806   (i) 3320   (j) 3636
4. (a) 642   (b) 1692   (c) 2860   (d) 1092
   (e) 2564   (f) 1578

Exercise 7E
1. (a) 840   (b) 620   (c) 960   (d) 1230   (e) 3420
   (f) 6080   (g) 90   (h) 200   (i) 280   (j) 240
   (k) 450   (l) 990
2. (a) 700   (b) 2500   (c) 1000   (d) 8700   (e) 4000
   (f) 6500   (g) 1500   (h) 5400   (i) 4000   (j) 6300
   (k) 2800   (l) 4800   (m) 3900   (n) 7000
   (o) 3000   (p) 9000
3. (a) 2000   (b) 4000   (c) 6000   (d) 9000   (e) 6000
   (f) 6000   (g) 8000   (h) 4000
4. (a) 840   (b) 1200   (c) 1120   (d) 1080   (e) 1710
   (f) 910   (g) 840   (h) 1150   (i) 2380   (j) 6400
   (k) 2040   (l) 1480

5. (a) 4920　(b) 3000　(c) 4560　(d) 7080　(e) 8010
　(f) 8560　(g) 8400　(h) 8000　(i) 9570　(j) 8680
6. (a) 6000　(b) 5400　(c) 7600　(d) 8000　(e) 7500
　(f) 5400　(g) 9600　(h) 7200　(i) 8800　(j) 8400
7. (a) 3680　(b) 3420　(c) 1820　(d) 3720　(e) 3300　(f) 3420
8. (a) 4560　(b) 9800　(c) 6900　(d) 6900　(e) 8720　(f) 9360

Exercise 7F
1. (a) 132　(b) 182　(c) 256　(d) 345　(e) 850
　(f) 798　(g) 1792　(h) 2752　(i) 3420　(j) 5712
2. (a) 242　(b) 713　(c) 429　(d) 516　(e) 736　(f) 714
3. (a) 350　(b) 612　(c) 1026　(d) 1608　(e) 2700　(f) 625
4. (a) 1008　(b) 1568　(c) 3234　(d) 4592　(e) 2037　(f) 5070

Exercise 7G
1. (a) 1512　(b) 1911　(c) 3430　(d) 3120　(e) 4688
　(f) 5185　(g) 7524　(h) 9747　(i) 9919　(j) 7250
　(k) 8848　(l) 10602　(m) 6358　(n) 7992　(o) 9504

Exercise 7H
1. 940　　2. 1248　　3. 420　　4. 1080
5. (a) 4320　(b) 720　(c) 1488　(d) 2250　(e) 4380

Exercise 8B
1. (a) 12 (b) 23 (c) 21 (d) 11 (e) 23 (f) 24 (g) 13 (h) 12
2. (a) 13　(b) 12　(c) 43　(d) 11
3. (a) 41　(b) 32　(c) 11　(d) 31

Exercise 8C
1. (a) 242 (b) 231 (c) 112 (d) 402 (e) 102 (f) 230 (g) 110 (h) 200
2. (a) 111　(b) 123　(c) 212　(d) 133
3. (a) 102　(b) 104　(c) 302　(d) 101
4. (a) 120　(b) 240　(c) 230　(d) 120
5. (a) 200　(b) 300　(c) 400　(d) 200
6. (a) 121　(b) 111　(c) 312　(d) 324
7. (a) 203　(b) 301　(c) 101　(d) 202
8. (a) 210　(b) 110　(c) 210　(d) 320
9. (a) 100　(b) 100　(c) 100　(d) 100

Exercise 8D
1. (a) 1234　(b) 1221　(c) 1231　(d) 2021　(e) 2001
　(f) 2030　(g) 4300　(h) 2000
2. (a) 1332　(b) 2312　(c) 3421　(d) 4241
3. (a) 1204　(b) 2031　(c) 2032　(d) 2102
4. (a) 2004　(b) 2003　(c) 2001　(d) 1001
5. (a) 4210　(b) 1310　(c) 1220　(d) 1110
6. (a) 2400　(b) 2100　(c) 2100　(d) 1100
7. (a) 3000　(b) 3000　(c) 2000　(d) 1000
8. (a) 2131　(b) 1323　(c) 2112　(d) 1111　(e) 4201
　(f) 3002　(g) 3100　(h) 1201

Exercise 8E
1. (a) 4, remainder 1; dividend = 2 × 4 + 1 = 9
　(b) 1, remainder 3;　dividend = 4 × 1 + 3 = 7
　(c) 11, remainder 3; dividend = 5 × 11 + 3 = 58
　(d) 11, remainder 2; dividend = 7 × 11 + 2 = 79
2. (a) 122, remainder 1　　　(b) 111, remainder 1
　(c) 1233, remainder 1　　(d) 1231, remainder 2
3. (a) 32, R = 1　(b) 32, R = 2　(c) 21, R = 3
　(d) 30, R = 1　(e) 30, R = 2
4. (a) 122, R = 1　(b) 321, R = 1　(c) 323, R = 1
　(d) 121, R = 3　(e) 111, R = 3
5. (a) 103, R = 1　(b) 102, R = 2　(c) 202,　R = 1
　(d) 100, R = 4　(e) 100, R = 3
6. (a) 340, R = 1　(b) 120, R = 2　(c) 120, R = 2
　(d) 110, R = 6　(e) 110, R = 5
7. (a) 4321, R = 1　(b) 2322, R = 1　(c) 1212, R = 1
　(d) 4312, R = 1　(e) 1221, R = 3
8. (a) 2012, R = 1　(b) 3202, R = 1　(c) 2011, R = 2
　(d) 1201, R = 2　(e) 1201, R = 1
9. (a) 4130, R = 1　(b) 1210, R = 2　(c) 3210, R = 2
　(d) 1100,　R = 5　(e) 3100, R = 1
10. (a) 4002, R = 1　(b) 1001, R = 3　(c) 1001, R = 2
　(d) 2000, R = 3　(e) 1000, R = 4

Exercise 9A
1. (a) 26, R = 0.　Dividend = 2 x 26 + 0 = 52
　(b) 14, R = 2.　Dividend = 3 x 14 + 2 = 44
　(c) 19, R = 0.　Dividend = 4 x 19 + 0 = 76
　(d) 13, R = 3.　Dividend = 5 x 13 + 3 = 68
2. (a) 263, R = 0　(b) 64, R = 2　(c) 1602, R = 0　(d) 309, R = 1
3. (a) 14, R = 0　(b) 14, R = 2　(c) 17, R = 0
　(d) 13, R = 0　(e) 12, R = 0

4. (a) 26, R = 1　(b) 23, R = 3　(c) 13, R = 2
　(d) 19, R = 1　(e) 12, R = 3
5. (a) 271, R = 0　(b) 263, R = 0　(c) 231, R = 2
　(d) 121, R = 2　(e) 129, R = 0
6. (a) 112, R = 0　(b) 325, R = 0　(c) 105, R = 2
　(d) 102, R = 0　(e) 106, R = 4
7. (a) 91, R = 0　(b) 67, R = 1　(c) 65, R = 0
　(d) 65, R = 1　(e) 84, R = 4
8. (a) 230, R = 3　(b) 120, R = 4　(c) 40, R = 5
　(d) 120, R = 0　(e) 66, R = 6
9. (a) 919, R = 0　(b) 968, R = 2　(c) 727, R = 0
　(d) 715, R = 0　(e) 913, R = 5
10. (a) 702, R = 4　(b) 907, R = 0　(c) 909, R = 0
　(d) 850, R = 4　(e) 970, R = 0
11. (a) 18, R = 0　(b) 16, R = 0　(c) 18, R = 3　(d) 12, R = 5
12. (a) 152, R = 0　(b) 356, R = 0　(c) 171, R = 2　(d) 119, R = 2
13. (a) 427, R = 0　(b) 112, R = 3　(c) 104, R = 2　(d) 109, R = 0
14. (a) 67, R = 0　(b) 61, R = 3　(c) 90, R = 0　(d) 70, R = 2
15. (a) 1837, R = 0　(b) 906, R = 0　(c) 1020, R = 5　(d) 1005, R = 0

Exercise 9B
1. (a) 10, R = 1　(b) 11, R = 0　(c) 45, R = 0　(d) 9, R = 10
2. (a) 11, R = 0　(b) 40, R = 9　(c) 32, R = 0　(d) 9, R = 2
3. (a) 11, R = 0　(b) 42, R = 10　(c) 30, R = 5　(d) 9, R = 8
4. (a) 11, R = 0　(b) 20, R = 4　(c) 52, R = 0　(d) 9, R = 7
5. (a) 20, R = 0　(b) 11, R = 0　(c) 33, R = 2　(d) 8, R = 6

Exercise 9C
3. 19　　　4. 12　　　5. 15, flowers left = 7
6. (a) 12　　(b) 14　　(c) 21　　(d) 12, flowers left = 4

Review Worksheet 3
1. (a) 70　(b) 329　(c) 372　(d) 4248　(e) 4347
2. (a) 1440　(b) 3640　(c) 5250　(d) 18630　(e) 7800
3. (a) 1536　(b) 4800　(c) 2921　(d) 7956　(e) 8667
4. (a) 19, R = 1; dividend = 2 × 19 x 1 = 39
　(b) 18, R = 3; dividend = 4 × 18 +3 = 75
　(c) 4, R = 0; dividend = 12 × 4 +0 = 48
　(d) 4, R = 1; dividend = 15 × 4 + 1 = 61
5. (a) 66, R = 0　(b) 103, R = 2　(c) 680, R = 3　(d) 409, R = 8

Exercise 14A
1. (a) 500 p　(b) 6800 p　(c) 9000 p　(d) 850 p　(e) 1100 p　(f) 8775 p
2. (a) Rs 32.25　(b) Rs 2.65　(c) Re 0.50　(d) Re 0.08
　(e) Rs 27.00　(f) Rs 453.25　(g) Rs 672.15
3. (a) 710　(b) 2500　(c) 7600　(d) 50.00　(e) 49.95　(f) 68.45

Exercise 14B
1. (a) 60 p　(b) Rs 1 25 p　(c) Rs 80　(d) Rs 37 70 p　(e) Rs 108 20 p
2. (a) Rs 360.85　(b) Rs 704.00　(c) ₹ 630.25　(d) ₹ 1061.00
3. (a) Rs 3479.90　(b) Rs 289.80　(c) Rs 826.10　(d) Rs 7902.00
4. (a) Rs 134.20　(b) Rs 695.60　(c) ₹ 6618.00
　(d) Rs 238.55　(e) ₹ 8221.15
5. (a) 35 p　(b) Rs 45　(c) Rs 29 20 p
　(d) Rs 28 75 p　(e) Rs 47 75 p
6. (a) Rs 734.80　(b) Rs 575.15　(c) ₹ 4059.35　(d) ₹ 6250.80
7. (a) Rs 125.30　(b) Rs 550.35　(c) ₹ 1177.60
8. (a) Rs 111.30　(b) Rs 80.75　(c) ₹ 4645.50

Exercise 14C
1. (a) 75 p　(b) 300 p　(c) 180 p　(d) 2100 p
　(e) 72　(f) Rs 48　(g) Rs 180　(h) Rs 1000
2. (a) Rs 46.80　(b) Rs 61.00　(c) Rs 2.70　(d) Rs 580.00
　(e) Rs 525.90　(f) Rs 635.25　(g) Rs 404.00　(h) Rs 995.70
3. (a) Rs 6.65　(b) Rs 288.00　(c) Rs 3.75　(d) Rs 64.00
　(e) ₹ 345.15　(f) ₹ 584.50　(g) ₹ 1351.95　(h) ₹ 4536.25

Exercise 14D
1. (a) 5 p　(b) 100 p　(c) Rs 7　(d) Rs 6
　(e) Rs 8　(f) Rs 6　(g) Rs 9　(h) Rs 100
2. (a) Rs 7.10　(b) Rs 7.05　(c) Rs 7.01　(d) Rs 8.10
3. (a) 2 rupees 20 paise　(b) 2 rupees 10 paise　(c) 6 rupees 10 paise
4. (a) Rs 12.00　(b) Rs 9.00　(c) Rs 5.01　(d) 16.05
　(e) ₹ 6.05　(f) ₹ 9.05　(g) ₹ 9.05　(h) ₹ 12.15

Exercise 14E
1. Tea Rs 40 50 p + Sugar Rs 39 50 p + Milk Rs 22 00 p = Rs 102 00 p
2. Rs 125　　3. Rs 90　　4. Rs 60
5. (a) Chair Rs 1200 00 p + Table Rs 2570 00 p + Cupboard Rs 5895 00 p
　 = Rs 9665 00 p
　(b) Rs 402.00　(c) Rs 825　(d) Rs 5　(e) ₹ 1005.55　(f) ₹ 972　(g) 31

Review Worksheet 4

3. (a) one (b) four (c) six, twelve
   (d) two, one, two (e) 0.50 (f) 6250
   (g) 73 (h) 4 (i) 5 (j) 1
4. (a) Rs 161.30 (b) Rs 4747.35 5. (a) Rs 32.50 (b) Rs 2817.75
6. (a) Rs 482.65 (b) Rs 3257.10
7. (a) Rs 27.10 (b) 13 rupees 10 paise

Exercise 15B

1. (a) 240 (b) 48 (c) 21 (d) 120 (e) 420 (f) 168
2. (a) 360 minutes (b) 252 minutes (c) 300 seconds
   (d) 575 seconds (e) 192 hours (f) 263 hours
   (g) 35 days (h) 53 days (i) 270 days
   (j) 104 days (k) 52 hours (l) 492 minutes
   (m) 336 hours (n) 111 days
3. 26 January, 15 August, 5 September, 2 October, 14 November
4. Safety pin, Light bulb, Aeroplane, Television, Computer mouse
5. 15 December 2003, 4 July 2005, 7 February 2009,
   21 May 2009, 8 March 2010
6. 2005 7. 1907 8. 3 January

Exercise 16A

1. (a) 300 cm (b) 700 cm (c) 1700 cm (d) 5600 cm
2. (a) 590 cm (b) 2875 cm (c) 3518 cm (d) 4709 cm (e) 9907 cm
3. (a) 4 m (b) 6 m (c) 10 m (d) 35 m
4. (a) 3 m 18 cm (b) 6 m 49 cm (c) 5 m 8 cm (d) 13 m 42 cm
   (e) 75 m 84 cm (f) 20 m 6 cm
5. (a) 4000 m (b) 6000 m (c) 82000 m (d) 90000 m
6. (a) 3143 m (b) 6375 m (c) 4072 m (d) 9005 m (e) 6007 m
7. (a) 3 km (b) 5 km (c) 6 km (d) 8 km
8. (a) 3 km 512 m (b) 2 km 589 m (c) 6 km 342 m
   (d) 5 km 600 m (e) 4 km 80 m (f) 7 km 4 m

Exercise 16B

1. (a) 65 cm (b) 832 m (c) 95 km (d) 64 m 80 cm (e) 6 km 422 m
2. (a) 70 cm (b) 95 cm (c) 63 cm (d) 96 cm
   (e) 832 m (f) 431 m (g) 63 km (h) 647 km
3. (a) 165 m 73 cm (b) 684 m 99 cm (c) 99 m 50 cm (d) 438 m 70 cm
4. (a) 59 km 810 m (b) 542 km 900 m
   (c) 894 km 267 m (d) 797 km 744 m
5. (a) 18 cm (b) 29 m (c) 48 km (d) 26 m 17 cm (e) 36 km 264 m
6. (a) 25 cm (b) 8 cm (c) 59 cm (d) 47 cm
   (e) 199 m (f) 14 km (g) 19 km (h) 377 km
7. (a) 16 m 16 cm (b) 15 m 34 cm (c) 57 m 12 cm
8. (a) 39 km 379 m (b) 39 km 262 m (c) 11 km 548 m

Exercise 16C

1. (a) 92 cm (b) 114 m (c) 216 km (d) 64 m 84 cm (e) 228 km 462 m
2. (a) 54 cm (b) 74 cm (c) 84 cm (d) 294 m (e) 928 m (f) 835 m
   (g) 102 km (h) 245 km (i) 1665 km (j) 714 km
3. (a) 74 m 98 cm (b) 196 m 98 cm (c) 215 m 85 cm (d) 312 m 78 cm
4. (a) 512 km 968 m (b) 128 km 768 m
   (c) 116 km 846 m (d) 216 km 975 m

Exercise 16D

1. (a) 16 cm (b) 9 cm (c) 17 cm (d) 19 m (e) 93 m (f) 86 m
   (g) 59 m (h) 75 km (i) 87 km (j) 97 km
2. (a) 14 m 28 cm (b) 132 m 15 cm (c) 121 m 18 cm (d) 41 m 8 cm
3. (a) 13 km 4 m (b) 12 km 71 m (c) 21 km 15 m (d) 302 km 160 m

Exercise 17A

1. (a) 3000 g (b) 7000 g (c) 8000 g (d) 9000 g
2. (a) 5700 g (b) 3060 g (c) 2097 g (d) 4009 g (e) 3608 g (f) 1005 g
3. (a) 4 kg (b) 2 kg (c) 7 kg (d) 9 kg
4. (a) 7 kg 629 g (b) 6 kg 903 g (c) 8 kg 200 g (d) 7 kg 4 g
   (e) 1 kg 357 g (f) 3 kg 48 g

Exercise 17B

1. (a) 825 g (b) 630 g (c) 87 kg 853 g (d) 624 kg 830 g
2. (a) 687 g (b) 737 g (c) 741 g
3. (a) 9230 kg (b) 481 kg (c) 5041 kg
4. (a) 102 kg 800 g (b) 844 kg 777 g (c) 220 kg 407 g (d) 435 kg 477 g
   (e) 2241 kg 243 g (f) 8780 kg 815 g
5. (a) 115 g (b) 186 kg (c) 7 kg 199 g (d) 280 kg 391 g
6. (a) 341 g (b) 546 g (c) 587 g (d) 291 g
7. (a) 534 kg (b) 375 kg (c) 2696 kg (d) 1256 kg
8. (a) 6 kg 708 g (b) 29 kg 188 g (c) 29 kg 305 g (d) 450 kg 455 g
   (e) 356 kg 555 g (f) 3691 kg 925 g

Exercise 17C

1. (a) 426 g (b) 2375 kg (c) 9 kg 828 g (d) 256 kg 592 g
2. (a) 144 g (b) 875 g (c) 960 g (d) 981 g

3. (a) 261 kg (b) 1760 kg (c) 3408 kg (d) 6556 kg
4. (a) 69 kg 765 g (b) 420 kg 875 g (c) 220 kg 872 g (d) 210 kg 912 g
   (e) 3300 kg 984 g (f) 9735 kg 888 g

Exercise 17D

1. (a) 24 g (b) 61 g (c) 107 g (d) 99 g
2. (a) 12 kg (b) 272 kg (c) 102 kg (d) 1036 kg
3. (a) 12 kg 31 g (b) 16 kg 6 g (c) 20 kg 304 g (d) 105 kg 90 g
   (e) 114 kg 131 g (f) 20 kg 105 g (g) 109 kg 50 g (h) 72 kg 66 g

Exercise 18A

1. (a) 3000 mL (b) 7000 mL (c) 6000 mL (d) 8000 mL
2. (a) 7400 mL (b) 3098 mL (c) 2045 mL (d) 9302 mL (e) 5005 mL
3. (a) 2 L (b) 3 L (c) 5 L (d) 7 L
4. (a) 1 L 745 mL (b) 4 L 512 mL (c) 2 L 500 mL (d) 4 L 70 mL
   (e) 8 L 102 mL (f) 3 L 5 mL

Exercise 18B

1. (a) 810 mL (b) 823 L (c) 81 L 820 mL (d) 624 L 581 mL
2. (a) 661 mL (b) 835 mL (c) 500 mL
3. (a) 975 L (b) 210 L (c) 663 L (d) 658 L
4. (a) 15 L 523 mL (b) 242 L 890 mL (c) 87 L 826 mL (d) 869 L 670 mL
   (e) 640 L 165 mL (f) 3850 L 936 mL
5. (a) 479 mL (b) 235 L (c) 19 L 228 mL (d) 29 L 435 mL
6. (a) 183 mL (b) 435 mL (c) 467 mL (d) 393 mL
7. (a) 54 mL (b) 257 L (c) 30 L (d) 1761 L
8. (a) 3 L 345 mL (b) 13 L 87 mL (c) 112 L 568 mL (d) 13 L 106 mL
   (e) 635 L 12 mL (f) 3987 L 209 mL

Exercise 18C

1. (a) 868 mL (b) 736 L (c) 75 L 885 mL (d) 675 L 775 mL
2. (a) 750 mL (b) 990 mL (c) 795 mL (d) 756 mL
3. (a) 301 L (b) 3216 L (c) 1075 L (d) 4128 L
4. (a) 42 L 948 mL (b) 144 L 712 mL
   (c) 1000 L 840 mL (d) 1785 L 700 mL

Exercise 18D

1. (a) 13 mL (b) 98 mL (c) 103 mL (d) 102 mL
2. (a) 42 L (b) 45 L (c) 72 L (d) 129 L
3. (a) 1 L 9 mL (b) 15 L 70 mL (c) 17 L 204 mL (d) 19 L 95 mL
   (e) 36 L 56 mL (f) 103 L 54 mL (g) 115 L 70 mL (h) 69 L 308 mL

Exercise 19A

1. 16 m 65 cm 2. 2 m 15 cm 3. 51 km 960 m 4. 2 m 15 cm
5. 34 km 750 m 6. 8 km 7. 30 cm 8. 120 km

Exercise 19B

1. 1250 g (= 1 kg 250 g) 2. 13 kg 3. 1200 g (= 1 kg 200 g) 4. 125 g
5. 11 kg 750 g 6. 24 kg 7. 288 kg 960 g 8. 3 kg 50 g

Exercise 19C

1. 2 L 750 mL 2. 321 L 600 mL 3. 20 L 4. 150 mL 5. 108 L 600 mL
6. 15 mL 7. 12 L 25 mL 8. 210 L

Exercise 20A

1.

Sweet		Total
🍬	卌 //	7
🍭	////	4
🍪	卌 /	6
🔍	////	4

2.

Total
4
13
7

3. (a) Piyush (b) Harsh (c) 25 kg (d) Two (e) Two
4. 110 5. 180 6. (a) 30 and 21 (b) 102 (c) Fancy dress
7. (a) 50 (b) 75 (c) 120 8. (a) 210 (b) 30 (c) False (d) True
9. 300 600 550 500 350
   April May June July August

10.

							5 children
Mountain	☺ ☺ ☺ ☺				Mountain		
Beach	☺ ☺ ☺ ☺		☺		Beach		
Desert	☺ ☺				Desert		5 children

Review Worksheet 5

1. 5:10, 8:20, 2:15, 6:35, 11:55
2. (a) 180 (b) 120 (c) 28 (d) 90 (e) 540 (f) 336 (g) 700
   (h) 8 (i) 4 (j) 6000 (k) 5000 (l) 6 (m) 9 (n) 2000
3. (a) 185 minutes (b) 181 hours (c) 162 days (d) 26 days
   (e) 2032 mL (f) 1 L 357 mL (g) 8300 g (h) 7 kg 168 g
   (i) 920 cm (j) 6 m 1 cm
4.

Number of students

						5 children
Bus						
Scooter						

5. (a) 140 km 452 m (b) 8 kg 529 g
   (c) 232 L 768 mL
6. 504 kg 840 g 7. 81 mL

156